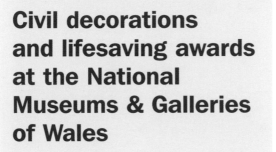

# For Those In Peril

## Civil decorations and lifesaving awards at the National Museums & Galleries of Wales

**Edward Besly**

First published in 2004 by National Museums & Galleries
of Wales, Cathays Park, Cardiff, CF10 3NP, Wales.

© National Museum of Wales

ISBN 0 7200 0546 9

| | |
|---|---|
| Production: | *Mari Gordon* |
| Design: | *The Info Group* |
| Printed by: | *MWL Print Group* |

*There are honours which are accorded men who seek glory at the cannon's mouth, in a good cause such may be desirable, but this facing, this fighting an unseen, lurking deadly foe, to save life, is a heroism of a more exalted kind.*

*From a manuscript memoir relating to the Beith family (NMGW 80.9H/4b See pp.15-16)*

## Acknowledgements

I am indebted to many people who have so willingly and helpfully answered questions from one for whom writing about medals represents a new departure, notably: Chris Delaney, Carmarthen; Roy Lewis, Pembrokeshire; Brian Wead, Royal National Lifeboat Institution; John David, Porthcawl; Elaine Hood, Illustrated London News Picture Library; E. G. Williams, Liverpool Shipwreck & Humane Society; David Dykes, Dorchester; Pamela Willis, Order of St John; Diana Coke and Christopher Tyler, Royal Humane Society; Bruce W. Anderson and Margaret Irvine, Carnegie Hero Fund Trust; P.A. Perry JP, Abercwmboi; Joanne Ratcliffe, RAF Museum, Hendon; Kevin Clancy and Graham Dyer, the Royal Mint. Carl Smith, Swansea, F.C. Hortop, Barry and Allan J. Woodliffe, Graigwen, had provided information previously, relating to the *Harriett* (1), Gordon Bastian and Bert Craig respectively. I also thank my NMGW colleagues Carolyn Charles and Ceri Thompson (Department of Industry); Sioned Wyn Hughes (Department of Social & Cultural History); Beth McIntyre (Department of Art); Jim Wild, Tony Hadland and Kevin Thomas (Photography Department); Tony Daly (Department of Archaeology & Numismatics) for the maps; Mari Gordon and Geraint MacDonald (Publications & Design Department).

John Gubb and Margaret Purves GC commented very helpfully on sections of the draft text. Allan Stanistreet read the whole and suggested several improvements as well as drawing my attention to the photographs of James Dally (25) and R. R. Williams (34). My colleagues Richard Brewer, Sally Carter and Eurwyn Wiliam also read the draft text, to its distinct benefit. Errors and inadequacies that may remain are mine.

I am grateful to the following organisations for permission to reproduce copyright and other material in their care: The Illustrated London News Picture Library (5,24,32,33); The Shropshire Regimental Museum (18);The National Archives: Public Record Office (27,28,47,51); The Royal Mint (29); National Library of Wales/The Western Mail and Echo (62,81); The RAF Museum, Hendon (63); Imperial War Museum (72); The Government Art Collection (74,75); The Glamorgan Record Office/South Wales Police (77,78). Parliamentary copyright material from Hansard is reproduced with the permission of the Controller of Her Majesty's Stationery Office on behalf of Parliament. Special thanks are due to Kenneth Williams for the use of photographs from his collection relating to holders of the Victoria Cross and George Cross (50,54,57,71,82,84); David Carpenter (34); John Gubb (36); Miss Margaret Pantling (46).

Every attempt has been made to contact copyright holders. Where unsuccessful, the National Museums & Galleries of Wales would appreciate any information that would enable it to do so.

# Contents

# A Summary Chronology

| | |
|---|---|
| **1774** | Royal Humane Society and Medal |
| **1787** | The Proclamation Society |
| **1824** | Royal National Lifeboat Institution founded; medal, 1825 |
| **1836** | Lloyd's Medal for Saving Life at Sea |
| **1839** | Liverpool Shipwreck & Humane Society founded; medal, 1844 |
| **1841** | (Sea Gallantry Medal (Foreign Services)) |
| **1854** | The Board of Trade Sea Gallantry Medal |
| **1866** | The Albert Medal (sea) |
| **1874** | Order of St John Lifesaving Medal |
| **1877** | The Albert Medal (land) |
| **1894** | The Hong Kong Plague Medal |
| **1896** | SS *Drummond Castle* Medal |
| **1907** | The Edward Medal (mines) |

| | |
|---|---|
| **1908** | Carnegie Hero Fund Trust founded<br>The Messina Earthquake, 28 December; medal, 1910 |
| **1909** | The Edward Extension Medal (industry)<br>The King's Police Medal<br>Boy Scout Awards |
| **1922** | (The Empire Gallantry Medal) |
| **1923** | (*Daily Herald* Order of Industrial Heroism) |
| **1940** | The George Cross<br>The George Medal<br>(Empire Gallantry Medal revoked)<br>Lloyd's Medal for Bravery at Sea |
| **1949** | The last Albert and Edward Medals to living recipients |
| **1954** | (The Queen's Police Medal)<br>(The Queen's Fire Service Medal) |
| **1971** | The Albert Medal revoked<br>The Edward Medal revoked |
| **1974** | (The Queen's Gallantry Medal)<br><br>(Awards in brackets are not represented in the NMGW collection.) |

# Introduction

During the 1920s, the National Museum of Wales acquired a representative collection of military medals, thanks to donations from private collectors. Civil awards have been acquired more gradually, since 1931: the first specifically Welsh award, Isaiah Thomas's Albert Medal (13), entered the collection in 1933. Over the years there were occasional donations or purchases, but the revoking of the Albert and Edward Medals in favour of the George Cross in October 1971 transformed the Museum's holdings: five holders of the Albert Medal and two of the Edward Medal elected to present their medals to the Museum. Since then more donations and the occasional purchase at auction have broadened the collection's coverage.

At the heart of this national collection are ten Albert Medals and five Edward Medals, the most recently acquired of these being the Edward Medal of Arthur Morris (30), part of the collection of Big Pit: the National Mining Museum of Wales. The standard of action required for either award was very high, as the stories recounted here show: not for nothing was the Albert Medal described as the 'civilian Victoria Cross' and the Edward Medal the 'miners' VC'. Part of the Museum's purpose, as defined by its Royal Charter, is 'the complete illustration of the ... history and special industries of Wales'. Foremost amongst these has been coal mining, and a significant portion of the collection comprises awards for gallantry in incidents arising from this industry. A second group arises from disasters at sea, in coastal waters or other rescues from drowning. In three cases, coal mining and inundation went hand-in-hand: Tynewydd, Clydach Vale and Brynamman.

The collection includes notable landmarks: the first Albert Medals for land service (10-13), one of the first two Edward Medals (22) and the last Albert Medal to a living recipient (83).

This book aims to provide an illustrated account of the civil gallantry awards in the collections of the National Museums & Galleries of Wales, telling the stories of the individuals involved and the contexts of the deeds for which they were recognised. They also provide an insight into the evolution of the civil honours system and the official processes by which such awards came about. The arrangement is broadly chronological, based on the events themselves, though there is inevitably an element of compromise. I have quoted extensively (and in two cases fully) from the *London Gazette*, the citations in which often, but by no means always, provide the best condensed account of an incident; also from newspapers and other contemporary sources, notably the Home Office HO 45 series of files in The National Archives: Public Record Office. (Unless otherwise indicated, the relevant HO 45 file is the source of quotations relating to individual Albert and Edward Medal cases.) Some information has been acquired with the medals, gathered by previous researchers. The stories of Tynewydd, Hong Kong, Messina, Clydach Vale and Llanreath draw on published accounts, often augmented from other sources.

The medals themselves are mostly of high quality, both in design and manufacture, befitting their function as visible rewards for acts of high courage. Both the portraits of the sovereigns (the side visible when royal awards were worn) and the symbolic reverses that went with them were designed by artists of high calibre, among these the Wyon family (William, Benjamin, Leonard, etc.), who dominated nineteenth-century medal making, George William De Saulles and Gilbert Bayes. Most were made at the Royal Mint in London, at first as private commissions; the Mint came to take this work over as part of its official responsibilities during the 1850s. Others were struck by private firms such as Elkington (for instance, 9) and John Pinches (59-60). With a few exceptions, the medals were made by careful striking between engraved dies, with bars or loops for suspension applied afterwards. However, the first award, from 1823 and by an unknown maker, is a good example of the genre of one-off engraved medals of the time, typified in Wales by extensive series of Cymreigyddion and Eisteddfod awards. The Boy Scouts' crosses, which consciously imitate the military Victoria Cross, were cast by Collins of London. The Albert Medal is in a class of its own, a complicated jewel-like creation with sixty-six component parts. An engraved inscription on the reverse names the recipient and date of the incident. At first the medal was manufactured by Phillips of 23 Cockspur Street, London, but its production was transferred to the Royal Mint in 1902. Many of the other medals are engraved on their edges, sometimes simply with details of the recipient, and sometimes with supplementary information (notably 9!). These edge inscriptions are quoted in the captions in single inverted commas.

The title of the book was inspired by Whiting's hymn 'Eternal father, strong to save …' and although this primarily refers to the sea, all of the awards described here relate to men and women who have gone out of their way to help 'those in peril', wherever this may have occurred. The collection provides a coherent view of British civil awards of the nineteenth and twentieth centuries and continues to develop as opportunity permits: George Calder's Sea Gallantry Medal (8) was acquired a matter of days before the text of this book was due to be completed. Individual specimens are held by several departments and branches of NMGW, as indicated. Where no location is given, a specimen forms part of the collection held by the Department of Archaeology & Numismatics at the National Museum & Gallery in Cardiff. If no donation or bequest is indicated, the specimen has been acquired by purchase.

# A Dangerous Coast

The extensive coastline of Wales (over 1,500 km) is for the most part rocky and exposed to the force of the prevailing westerly winds coming off the Atlantic Ocean. It is littered with shipwrecks – over 3,000 losses have been recorded. A Roman anchor stock of the second-first centuries BC found off Porth Felen, Lleyn Peninsula, and an early twelfth-century AD Viking decorated sword guard from the Smalls Rocks off St David's Head, Pembrokeshire, provide us with evidence of early disasters. Artefacts from the *Ann Francis* of King's Lynn, which came to grief in December 1583, continue to be found near Margam on the west Glamorgan coast. King Charles II's yacht *Mary* was wrecked on the Skerries, Anglesey, on 25 March 1675. The many incidents no doubt gave rise to numerous examples of personal bravery, but these are lost to us. From the eighteenth century, however, and particularly during the nineteenth, such incidents came to be recorded, both in local newspapers and by societies formed to encourage life-saving skills and to recognise and reward individual gallantry. Rewarding bravery in saving life at sea and elsewhere was, for instance, one of the objects of the 'charitable and benevolent' gentlemen's association, the Anglesey Druidical Society, founded in 1772.

The Proclamation Society was established by William Wilberforce to encourage the implementation of King George III's Proclamation for the 'Encouragement of Virtue and for the Prevention of Vice, Profaneness and Immorality' (1 June 1787). Carmarthen's was the local chapter for the Diocese of St David's and made awards for a range of virtuous activities, including services at shipwrecks. David Lewis of St Ishmael's, for instance, was given £3 3s for his 'great humanity' in helping sailors and passengers of the brig *William*, wrecked on Cefn Sidan sands, 10 September 1816, carrying seal skins and oil from Newfoundland to Bristol.

The medal illustrated here speaks for itself. The brig *Harriett* was on passage from Dublin to Barbados and Trinidad with linen, provisions, butter and porter, when she struck a rock off St David's Head, drifting on her beam ends for twelve hours. The master, William Kilhier, the crew and one passenger were saved, though there was one fatality, M.L. O'Reilly. In April, Messrs Starbuck and Co, Lloyd's agents at Milford, were instructed to present £20 to the boatmen of St David's for the rescue.

Nathaniel Phillips Bland (1769?-1830), of Upper Treleddyn near St David's, was a local landowner, 'a man, possessed of rare endowments of mind, dignified manners, inflexible integrity, unfeigned benevolence with every social and amiable virtue' according to his epitaph. One of his sisters, Dora (1761-1816) achieved national fame as Mrs Jordan, the leading comic actress of the day and mistress of the Duke of Clarence (who later became King William IV).

1. **Proclamation Society Carmarthen**
medal engraved to N.P. Bland; brig *Harriett*,
St David's Head, 21st February 1823.
Silver, 43 mm; hallmarked London, 1823
*Museum of Welsh Life (38.324/1)*

# James Pearse

'(Voted) the silver medal and 2*l*. [£2] each to James Pearse, Thomas Pearse, John Jones, pilots, and George Clark, seaman, in acknowledgement of their gallant services in putting off in a boat and rescuing 3 out of 4 men of the crew of the schooner *Trevaunance*, of St Agnes, which was wrecked, during an easterly gale, off Porthcawl, on the 29th March. After striking, the vessel almost immediately sank, when the crew, 4 in number, took to the mast head, where they remained for several hours, before they were seen from land. When the boat's crew were within half a mile of the wreck, they found that they could not approach her, owing to the heavy sea that was breaking over the sands. At last, when quite dark, and seeing that unless they then made the attempt, an hour or less would seal the poor creatures' fate, as the tide was close up to them, the boat dashed into the surf and took the shipwrecked men, now reduced to three, from their most perilous position on the cross-tree, to which they had clung for sixteen hours.' (From *The Life-Boat*, the magazine of the Royal National Lifeboat Institution, 1 October, 1857.)

The *Trevaunance* was carrying a cargo of copper ore from St Ives to Swansea.

The RNLI was founded on 4 March 1824, as the National Institution for the Preservation of Life from Shipwreck, and rapidly acquired a royal patron in King George IV. One of its first resolutions provided for the giving of medals or of monetary awards to those rescuing lives. The King's portrait graced the new medals, which were of gold or silver, and continued to do so until well into Queen Victoria's reign. The medal was designed and made by William Wyon, then second engraver at the Royal Mint, who included a self-portrait – the sailor on the reverse helping the shipwrecked victim. The Institution had in 1854 changed its name, to the 'Royal National Life-Boat Institution – founded in 1824 for the Preservation …' etc. and in 1860 was granted a Charter of Incorporation by Queen Victoria.

There were further local wrecks on Kenfig Sands in December 1858 and January 1860. The Porthcawl Lifeboat Station opened in April 1860; it closed in 1902 with the cessation of commercial trade locally. An inshore lifeboat has been based at Porthcawl since 1965 to assist recreational users of the sea and local coastline who get into difficulties. In 1995, Stuart Roberts of the Porthcawl boat was awarded the RNLI Silver Medal for outstanding bravery during the rescue of a seventeen-year-old surfer on 30 December 1994. Helmsman Nick Beale has received the Bronze Medal for saving a fisherman swept off the pier on 2 February 2002, a service carried out in mountainous seas with winds gusting to force ten.

2. **Royal National Lifeboat Institution, Silver Medal, type I**
'MR JAMES PEARSE. VOTED 7TH MAY 1857'
*(95.66H/1)*

# Thomas Rees

'(Voted) the silver medal of the Institution to Mr THOMAS M. REES, in acknowledgement of his gallant and skilful conduct in saving, at the risk of his life, by being lowered down some high cliffs, during the very dark and stormy night of the 5th Jan. last, 4 men from the schooner *Two Brothers*, of Holyhead, which was wrecked on the Pembrokeshire coast.'
(From *The Life-Boat*, 1 July, 1867.)

Thomas Rees, a local man, was instrumental in rescuing the four men at Pointz Castle Farm, near Solva in St Bride's Bay, after the boat in which they had put off from the schooner was itself wrecked.

3. **Royal National Lifeboat Institution, Silver Medal, type II**
'MR THOMAS MORTIMER REES voted 7th Feby 1867'
*(95.66H/2)*

In 1862 a new obverse for the medal was approved, designed by L.C. Wyon and depicting the Society's royal Patroness.

4. **St Bride's Bay**, pencil drawing by J. Gibbs, 1830 *NMGW, Department of Art*

**5. 'Rescue of the fishermen by the lifeboat Sunlight No.1 at Llandudno'**
(*ILN* Oct 19, 1889) *Illustrated London News Picture Library*

'Oct.7.- Llandudno – *Sunlight No. 1* Life-boat This life-boat, manned by its efficient crew, rendered its first service in saving life during a heavy gale which prevailed along the coast. Early in the morning two fishing trawlers from Hoylake, the *Perseverance*, Edward Smith, master, and the *Ellen and Ann*, Joseph Beck, master, anchored in Llandudno Bay about three miles from the shore. At about 9.30 it was observed that the *Perseverance* had hoisted a distress signal. The Life-boat, fully manned, was quickly launched in front of the South Parade, the boat being in charge of Mr. RICHARD JONES, coxswain. The launch was well managed, and as the boat put off in the tremendous sea which was running, hundreds of persons who had gathered on the parade gave a hearty cheer. In order to procure a better headway, and get a little shelter from the gale, the boat was steered out near the pier.

The public also made for the pier, where a good view of proceedings was available. The Life-boat was soon near the *Perseverance*, but it was some time before the men were got off; eventually four men were landed from the vessel at the pier-head. The Life-boat then put out again to the *Ellen and Ann*, which had also hoisted a signal of distress, and landed four more hands on the beach, amid the cheers of the spectators. The behaviour of the new Life-boat exceeded all expectations, and the crew are greatly pleased with the way in which she passed through this very severe test, as she had to encounter a very heavy breaking sea. - Expense of service, 24*l*. 6s.' (From *The Life-Boat*, 1 May, 1890.)

A ten-oared self-righting lifeboat, *Sunlight No.1* was stationed at Llandudno, Gwynedd, from 1887 to 1902, one of two such boats presented to the RNLI by Lord Lever (of Sunlight Soap fame). Also known as the Orme's Head lifeboat, 26 lives were saved during her service at Llandudno. *Sunlight No.2* was stationed at Brighton.

6. **Royal National Lifeboat Institution Gallantry Medal, type III, 1903**
Royal Mint unmounted specimen striking in bronze
*By bequest (two specimens, 48.126/43-44)*

With the accession of Edward VII, the RNLI medal was completely redesigned, by George William De Saulles, Engraver to the Royal Mint; the first award of the type was voted in August 1903. Use of the new reverse, which included a seated figure of Hope wishing 'God-speed' to the Coxswain-Superintendent of a lifeboat, was short lived: in 1912, Wyon's original was restored for the medals of King George V's reign. Actual awards in bronze were not introduced until 1917, and in 1937 the monarch's head on the obverse was replaced by that of Sir William Hillary, Bart, the Institution's founder.

7. **Board of Trade, Sea Gallantry Medal, bronze**
'Ezekiel Couth, "Madeline" wrecked in Torbay 11th Jany 1866'
*By private donation (32.131)*

Awarded for 'Gallantry' (risking one's life, as here) or 'Humanity' (providing services) in saving life at sea, this medal, 2 ¼ inches (58 mm) in diameter, was instituted through the Merchant Shipping Act of 1854, and issued in silver and bronze. The large size of the original medal precluded wear, but from 1904 it was replaced by smaller medals, 32 mm in diameter.

Couth's Sea Gallantry Medal was given to the National Museum by a relative who lived in Penarth. Records of the Sea Gallantry Medal from before 1887 no longer exist and little seems to be known of Ezekiel Couth's exploit in January 1866. However, a lengthy Board of Trade memorandum on rewards for saving life at sea drawn up that year includes the following:

'Board of Trade Bronze Medal: Jany 11 1866, During a violent gale a large number of vessels were wrecked in Torbay and many lives were lost. Several persons rendered valuable assistance in saving life but more especially C. Bartlett, E. Barler, A.G. Wyat & E. Couth. The first named was lowered over the cliff by means of a rope & the other men swam with ropes to vessels & by their exertions several lives were saved – while great risk was incurred in consequence of the strength of the gale & the darkness of the night. We gave to each of these men a Bronze Medal.' (*MT 9/29/W3202*)

This event provides an interesting link to the Albert Medal, established in March of the same year. One of the cases considered for the first awards was that of 'Bartlett and Couth (case 3)'. Christopher Bartlett was the outstanding figure in the Torbay rescue efforts, and his case reached a draft recommendation for the 'Albert Medal of the Second Class', from which we learn:

'About 33 lives were lost; but owing to the exertions of the Coast Guard Men, Fishermen, and others, about 190 lives were saved by means of lines and other assistance from the shore and 26 lives were saved by boats belonging to the wrecked vessels. Amongst those who exerted themselves in saving life was Christopher Bartlett, a fisherman ... the night was very dark and the weather thick with snow...' (*MT 9/32/M2120*, 11 March 1867).

Unfortunately, the new medal was not to be retrospective: 'Bartlett's case is not to be included. This was before the date of the Warrant' (9 May 1867).

# George Calder

The *Annie Park*, a Barrow-registered schooner en route from London to Lancaster was stranded and lost on St Govan's Head, Pembrokeshire, in a south-easterly gale, force nine. Calder, a Commissioned Boatman, HM Coastguard, descended the cliff to reach the wreck, crawling along a sloping ledge of rock two feet wide.

He reached two survivors and assisted in sending them to the top using lifelines and cliff ladder apparatus.

Calder received the silver medal and £2, and another boatman, Thomas Grills, the bronze medal and £1. The medals, approved by the King, were presented by the Tenby District Office of HM Coastguard.

8. **Sea Gallantry Medal, silver, Edward VII**; 'GEORGE CALDER. WRECK OF THE "ANNIE PARK" 2ND JANUARY 1906'
**British War Medal, 1914-20**; '118026 G. CALDER. C.P.O. R.N.'
**Royal Navy, Long Service and Good Conduct Medal, Victoria Second Type**; 'GEORGE CALDER, BOATMAN, H.M. COAST GUARD' *(2003.30H/1-3)*

# William Owen

The barque *Hermine*, registered in Liverpool, was en route from Peru to Liverpool with a cargo of sugar when she was wrecked at Porth-y-garan, Holy Island, off the Isle of Anglesey.

'A silver medal each to William Owen and Evan Owen, for having, at some risk, assisted to rescue the crew of the barque "Hermine", 16 in all, the said vessel having been wrecked in foggy weather on the rocks near Rhoscolyn, Holyhead Island on the 16th June, 1890.' (From the Society's 52nd *Annual Report*, for the year ended 1st July 1891.)

The RNLI, too, gave a financial reward to some unnamed men, one of them presumably William Owen, who rescued her crew:

'June 16. Four men rescued, by means of lines from the shore, the crew of sixteen men from the barque *Hermine*, of Liverpool, which had struck on the rocks and sunk at Porth y Garron, Anglesey, in a breeze from the S.W., a moderate sea, and thick weather. – Reward, 1*l*. 10s.' (From *The Life-Boat*, May 1, 1891.)

The Liverpool Shipwreck & Humane Society was founded in 1839 to administer the balance remaining from emergency funds, raised in the wake of a hurricane in the Irish Sea on 7-8 January to afford relief to the sufferers and to reward those who had saved life. Like the Sea Gallantry Medal, the Society's first medal, instituted in 1844, was (at 54 mm diameter) not intended for wear. A smaller oval medal of 1867 was in its turn soon replaced by the familiar 'small' circular type (1874–5), 38 mm in diameter and worn suspended from a blue ribbon. The Society produced a series of medals – fire, swimming proficiency, a general medal – as well as two for specific incidents, the Camp & Villaverde Medal (1847) and the Bramley-Moore Medal (1872). At the time of writing, the Society has awarded 74 gold, 2,799 silver and

2,104 bronze medals or bars for marine rescues, as well as many framed parchments and certificates. While most of the cases of bravery today are reported by Chief Constables, Chief Fire Officers, etc., many of the early cases relate to rescues all over the world, reported by shipping companies, provided that the vessel was Liverpool-registered.

9a. **Liverpool Shipwreck & Humane Society, Marine Medal in silver**
'WM OWEN FOR ASSISTING TO SAVE THE CREW (16 IN ALL) OF BARQUE HERMINE WRECKED ON HOLYHEAD ISLAND JUNE 16 / 1890'
*Museum of Welsh Life, by private donation (48.309)*

**9b. William Owen's Liverpool Shipwreck & Humane Society medal**,
showing the reverse design, in its manufacturer's case.

# The Albert Medal

## and the

## Tynewydd Inundation

*Thank God for deeds of valour,*
*like this we now record!*
*Thank God for British Heroes*
*Who never wore a sword!*
*Thank God for willing workers*
*Where danger's self is seen*
*The love enduring all things;*
*Thank God for England's Queen.*

*From* Troedyrhiw Colliery: or, the Rescuers and the Rescued
*by John Harries, the 'Cornish miners' poet'*

**William Beith**

**Isaac Pride**

**Rees Thomas**

**Isaiah Thomas**

On 7 March 1866, a Royal Warrant announced a new decoration, to be known as the Albert Medal, for rewarding 'daring and heroic actions' by mariners and others in saving life at 'wrecks and other perils of the sea'. The decoration, to be 'highly prized and eagerly sought after', was initially of a single class, but only one medal had been awarded by the time a further warrant (12 April 1867) introduced a second class; in part, this was the result of a perceived need to ration the medal's award to preserve its desired status and the difficulty of setting the standards required for the First Class award, which came to be regarded as the civilian equivalent of the Victoria Cross (which had been instituted in 1856). Seven First Class medals were awarded during the first decade of its existence. In 1877, the award of the Albert Medal was extended to recognition of services on land, following a nine-day operation to rescue four men and a boy trapped by floodwaters in a South Wales colliery.

'It is difficult to imagine a form of death more appalling than that of slow starvation in the darkness of a tomb, and it is therefore no matter of surprise that the story of the imprisoned miners in South Wales should have sent a thrill of horror throughout the whole of the country, and that the successive telegrams which told of the noble heroism with which their comrades were labouring for their rescue should have been watched for with anxious eagerness, and perused with mingled feelings of hope and apprehension.' (From *The Graphic*, 28 April, 1877.)

Around 4 p.m. on 11 April 1877, as the working day drew to a close, Tynewydd Colliery, near Porth in the Rhondda Valley of South Wales, was inundated by water from abandoned workings nearby. Fourteen colliers were still underground. Of these, four drowned and two groups of five were trapped in compressed pockets of air above the floodwaters. One group was rescued the following morning, though one of the men was killed when the compressed air was suddenly released. The second group, four men and a boy, were further from safety; they had no food, and a supply of candles they found was to last them around three days. Two divers tried to reach them, without success; only on 16 April had enough water (over ten million gallons) been pumped from the mine for a rescue attempt to begin. Relays of miners tunnelled towards them through 114 feet (35 m) of coal. Finally, at 1 p.m. on 20 April, the group was released, weak but alive after nine days underground.

As colliery disasters went, the Tynewydd inundation was relatively small – five lives lost and nine saved. Twenty-one years earlier, an explosion in the neighbouring Cymmer Colliery had cost 114 lives. In 1879 an explosion at the Abercarn (Monmouthshire) pit was to kill 260. However, news of the Tynewydd disaster and the desperate and courageous rescue attempt attracted huge press and public interest and the electric telegraph ensured that the Government and even Queen Victoria herself were kept fully informed. Bulletins were posted in the Lobby of the House of Commons. Special supplements were published after the event by both *The Graphic* and *The Illustrated London News*.

Official recognition of the rescuers' courage was immediately raised at the highest level. On 23 April, Lord Beaconsfield raised with the Queen the question of extending the Albert Medal to cover gallantry on land, or the possibility of creating a new award, to be called the Victoria Medal. The decision was rapid: 'Her Majesty the Queen has been graciously pleased to intimate her intention of bestowing the Albert Medal … upon those humble men who hazarded their own lives in cutting through the coal to extricate their starving comrades.' (From *ILN*, 28 April 1877.)

But who was to pay for the new medals? Not the Board of Trade: 'We pay for the Albert Medals for saving life at sea. The money comes from the Mercantile Marine Fund … We cannot pay for yours as our authority only extends to the saving of life at sea. I take it that the Treasury will have to give your office special & written authority for the expenditure' (3 May). 'I have spoken to Mr Smith … he thinks the Treasury had better pay for them out of their miscellaneous vote in Class 7 of the Civil Service Estimates' (Treasury, 5 May) (*HO 45/63549A/6,7*). By 18 July, the Queen had approved specimens of each class of the 'land' medal: those of the 'First Class' cost £7 15s 0d and the 'Second Class', £3 7s 6d, including boxes and engraving but not, curiously, the ribands (*HO 45/63459A/8*).

On 4 August an estimated 30,000-40,000 people assembled 'on the hill near the Rocking-stone at Pontypridd' for a ceremony presided over by the Lord-Lieutenant of Glamorgan. Awards were presented from the *Daily Telegraph*, the Order of St John (see 35), the House of Commons and the British and Foreign Bible Society. The Lord Mayor of London presented monetary awards from the Mansion House Fund, amounting to £4,000. 'Finally, Lord Aberdare, by command of the Queen, bestowed the Albert Medal on certain of those who had rescued their fellow-workmen from the flooded colliery. After singing the National Anthem and giving shouts for the Queen, the assembly dispersed.' (From *ILN*, 11 August 1877.)

Like its maritime counterpart, the Albert Medal (Land) was of two classes. The *London Gazette* of 7 August 1877 listed three groups of awards: four men received the 'Albert Medal of the First Class'; and twenty-one 'Albert Medals of the Second Class' were divided between those who had cut the coal and colliery managers or owners who had played significant parts in the rescue. Each group is represented in the NMGW collection.

11. **Albert Medal, Land, First Class (No 3)**
Isaac Pride
*Department of Industry, by private donation (38.634)*

'First Class' Albert Medals were awarded to William Beith, Mechanical Engineer of Harris's Navigation Colliery, Quakers Yard; Isaac Pride, collier, of Llwyncelyn Colliery; Daniel Thomas, Colliery Proprietor, Brithwynydd; and John William Howell, collier of Ynyshir.

10. **Albert Medal, Land, First Class (No 2)**
William Beith
*(80.9H/1) See also 35 and 43*

'The rescuing operations [of the trapped five] consisted in driving through the barrier of coal thirty-eight yards in length, which intervened between the imprisoned men and the rescuers, and kept back a large quantity of water and compressed air. This task was commenced on Monday, April the 16th, and was carried on until Thursday, April the 19th without any great amount of danger being incurred by the rescuers; but at about one o'clock P.M. on that day, when only a few yards of barrier remained, the danger from an irruption of water, gas, and compressed air was so great as to cause the colliers to falter. It was at this juncture that the above-mentioned four men volunteered to resume the rescuing operations, the danger of which had been greatly increased by an outburst of inflammable gas under great pressure, and in such quantities as to extinguish the Davy lamps which were being used. The danger from gas continued at intervals until half-past three on the following morning, and from that time the above four men at great peril to their own lives continued the rescuing operations until three o'clock P.M. when the five imprisoned men were safely released.'
(*London Gazette*, 7 August 1877)

A fifth member of this final rescue party, Abraham Dodd (another Ynyshir collier) was omitted from the Tynewydd honours list, for reasons that have never been clear.

William Beith was a Scot, the second of seven sons of a miner from Wilsontown, all of whom made their livings through mining or engineering. He was also commended in April 1893 by the Chairman of the Great Western Colliery Company for 'the prompt manner in which you came forward, at so much personal risk, and for the great assistance you rendered, in the dangerous emergency which arose, in connection with the late sad calamity at our Colliery': a fire under a haulage engine at the colliery at Gyfeillion (Hopkinstown), Pontypridd on the 11th had cost 63 lives.

12. **Albert Medal, Land, Second Class (No 34)**
Rees Thomas, Collier, Tynewydd Colliery
*Department of Industry, by private donation (82.154l)*

'During the five days from April the 16th to April the 20th the above-named eleven men were at various times engaged in cutting through the barrier of coal separating them from the five imprisoned men, and while exposing their lives to the great danger which would have resulted from an outburst of compressed air and water, and to the danger which actually existed from the presence of large quantities of inflammable gas, continued to perform their work until the five men were safely rescued.'
(*London Gazette*)

This third list initially included James Thomas, owner and manager of Tynewydd Colliery, but his name was subsequently removed: he was at that time facing charges of manslaughter in connection with the inundation – of which he was eventually cleared.

The Albert Medal, unusually, did not bear the portrait of the monarch. It took the form of a composite jewel bearing the initials of Victoria and Albert on an enamelled ground. The ribbons of the Second Class awards were considerably narrower (5/8″) than those for the First Class (1 3/8″). At first, Albert Medals were individually numbered, a practice that seems to have ceased in the early 1880s.

**13. Albert Medal, Land, Second Class (No 21)**
Isaiah Thomas, Colliery manager, Brithwynydd Colliery
*Department of Industry, by private donation (33.266)*

'From Thursday, April the 12th, when the operations for the rescue were commenced, until Friday, April the 20th, when the intervening barrier of coal had been cut through and the imprisoned men released, the above-named eleven men were present at different times, and, while being of valuable service in the rescue, exposed their own lives to the great danger which would have attended an outburst of water and compressed air, or an explosion of the inflammable gas which at different times during the rescue escaped under great pressure and in dangerous quantities.' (*London Gazette*)

THE FLOODED COLLIERY AT TROEDYRHIW, PORTH

Old Cymmer Mine, from whence the Water Came.  GENERAL VIEW OF THE TYNEWYDD DISTRICT  The Flooded Mine

14. **Tynewydd Colliery,** from *The Graphic* NMGW, *Department of Industry*

15. **Tynewydd – rescued and some of the rescuers,** posed some time after. Isaac Pride is standing, sixth from left. The rescued, seated l. to r., are: David Jenkins, George Jenkins, the boy David Hughes, Moses Powell and John Thomas NMGW, *Department of Industry*

**16 a.** (*see overleaf*)

16. **Examples of awards in the form of silver plate**

*Department of Industry, by private donations:*

a. Ewer, *Presented to William Davies Esq / out of the Mansion House Welsh Miners' Fund / in recognition of services rendered at the inundation of / the Tynewydd Colliery, April 1877.* By Barnard & Sons Ltd, hallmarked London, 1876; height 388 mm; weight 1.15kg. *(56.455)*

William Davies was Manager of Coedcae Colliery, Trehafod.

b. Tankard, *Valour* (on scroll) / *Daily Telegraph Welsh Miners' Fund / Presented to / Mr Isaiah Thomas / for / gallant conduct.* By J.W. Benson Ltd, hallmarked London, 1877; height 117 mm; weight 313.6g. *(33.266/1)*

c. Tankard, *Valour* (on scroll) /*Daily Telegraph Welsh Miners' Fund / Presented to / Mr Thomas G. Davies / for / gallant conduct.* By J.W. Benson Ltd, hallmarked London, 1877; height 117 mm; weight 319.7g. *(55.235/2)*

d. Ewer, *Presented to / Thomas G. Davies, Esq. / out of the Mansion House / Welsh Miners' Fund / in recognition of his bravery / in saving life / at the inundation / of the Tyn(e)wydd Colliery 1877.* By Henry Holland, hallmarked London, 1877; height 215 mm; weight 850g. *(55.235/1)*

Thomas Gedrych Davies, of Tylacoch, colliery manager, also received the Albert Medal of the Second Class.

# Soldiering On

*'Soldiers as a rule are trained to destroy life, not to save it, this was a new role for our friend Tommy Atkins, but he has done it well.'*

E.J. Ackroyd, *Acting Chief Justice of Hong Kong, 28 September 1894, in* The Whitewash Brigade, *p. 88*

The value of military organization and training extends beyond the obvious one of discipline under fire. On numerous occasions, bodies of servicemen have performed invaluable work in assisting civil authorities to cope with natural or man-made disasters. The outbreak of foot-and-mouth disease in England and Wales in 2001 provided a recent example. Individual gallantry has been recognised in the normal way, for instance the Albert and Empire Gallantry Medals awarded to servicemen involved in rescuing survivors of the Quetta, Baluchistan (present-day Pakistan) earthquake of 31 May 1935. In two cases, the appropriate authorities saw fit to make a more general issue of special medals to commemorate the exceptional contributions made by British service personnel: the Hong Kong Plague of 1894 and the Messina earthquake, 1908.

17. **Community of Hong Kong: Silver Medal for services rendered during the Plague of 1894**
'PRIVATE J. MORRIS, S.L.I.'
*By private donation (22.295/108)*

Bubonic plague (*Yersinia pestis*), endemic in parts of China, spread to the southern port of Canton in January 1894, an outbreak that was to cost 40,000 lives. When on 5 May the plague reached the bustling British colony of Hong Kong, some eighty or so miles away, it spread rapidly, exacerbated by overcrowding, poor sanitation in parts of the city and by water shortages caused by abnormally dry weather.

The authorities sought volunteers for plague control measures and rapidly turned to the colony's military garrison. On 23 May, eight officers and 300 men of the 1st Battalion, King's Shropshire Light Infantry, all volunteers, took up their duties. They were to be augmented by men of the Royal Engineers, the Royal Navy and the local Police. Their work was 'to visit from house to house, to search for the sick and dead, to remove them and to

remove the accumulation of dust and filth, furniture and other effects and then to thoroughly disinfect and cleanse these houses. This work was always done with alacrity and never-failing good humour and it was done only as volunteers could do it' (Ackroyd). Infected clothing, bedding and other rubbish were burned; police protection was often needed. Four men volunteered to drive mortuary carts and fifty on 8 June for special fumigating duties in the Taipingshan district, part of which was ultimately demolished. Several of the volunteers themselves contracted the plague and one officer and one Private died of it. The Sanitary Board and the local business community supported the volunteers with coffee and tobacco, even 'a tot of rum ... a gift from Mr Abdullah'.

At the plague's height in early June, over 100 people were dying daily and the final figure was over 2,500. Plague remained endemic for several years, though never again on the same scale. On 28 September 1894 a public meeting at the City Hall considered what steps should be taken in recognition of services rendered to the community during the plague. A committee was appointed, which decided to award 'certain medals and pieces of plate'. The medals were designed by Frank Bowcher and struck in gold and silver by Allan Wyon. They were awarded to the SLI and other units, to the Police and to civilians. Permission was sought for the soldiers to wear the medals in uniform but, not being a service medal, this was denied. A second specimen in the Museum's collection was awarded to 'Private A.E. Gilbert, S.L.I.' (*private donation, 24.192/1*).

**18. Men of the King's Shropshire Light Infantry disinfecting houses in the Chinese Quarter.**
'Whitewash' (disinfecting solution) is being carried into a house on the right; note the boarded-up house, left foreground, marked 'DONE'.
*Shropshire Regimental Museum*

19. **Kingdom of Italy, Messina Earthquake 'Commemorative' Silver Medal, authorised in 1910**
unnamed.
*By private donation (31.466/4)*

'At 5.15 a.m. all hands disturbed by heavy earthquake shock causing great confusion on board, rushing on deck but being pitched dark & the air full of dust was unable to see anything. Same time tidal wave came over quay which raised the ship bodily turning adrift all moorings … the port anchor was let go with 30 fths [fathoms] cable, which held the ship in position … At 7 am the sky cleared when we found out the quay had collapsed & town destroyed …' *Log of* SS Afonwen, *Messina 28 December 1908* (*Glamorgan Archive Service*)

The earthquake that destroyed the Sicilian port of Messina killed tens of thousands, including virtually all of those responsible for administration and public order. Immediate assistance to survivors was provided by the crews of an Italian battleship and four British merchant ships that had survived in the harbour. As news of the disaster spread there was a massive international rescue effort. From its base in Malta, the Royal Navy dispatched ships carrying food, blankets and medical personnel and supplies. A field hospital and Army Service Corps field bakery followed. Together with sailors from the Italian, Russian, German, French and American fleets, rescue parties went ashore to dig in the ruins, care for and evacuate the injured, and to recover and bury the dead. The last survivors were located eighteen days after the earthquake. By the end of January 1909, Messina had ceased to exist as further tremors completed its destruction. The city was declared a prohibited area and its ruins were spread with quicklime. A major programme of reconstruction started in 1911.

King Victor Emanuel III and Queen Elena of Italy had rushed to Messina, arriving on 30 December. They stayed for three days inspecting relief work and thanking the foreigners who had come to aid their people. On 6 May 1909 a 'merit' medal was authorised by Royal Decree. Gold and silver medals were presented to institutions (40 mm diameter) and individuals (30 mm). Among British recipients of the 'small' silver medal were four crew members of the Cardiff-registered *SS Afonwen*: Thomas Owen, Eric Possert, James Vivian Reed and Henry Smith. Reed and Smith were awarded the Albert Medal (Land, Second Class) for a particularly dangerous rescue of children from a crumbling five-storey building; they, with the ship's master William Owen, also received the Order of the Crown of Italy.

By a second decree, dated 20 February 1910, the Italian King decided to award a 'commemorative' medal to every person of every nation who had contributed to the rescue effort. The allocation of these silver medals was characterised by muddle and delay, but the medals were received in November 1911.

Over 4,000 were distributed to men of the Royal Navy and Royal Marines and nearly 400 to British crews of eight merchant ships. Unlike the Hong Kong plague medals, wearing of the medals in uniform was permitted.

A second specimen of the 'Commemorative' medal was presented to the Museum in 1946, perhaps derived from a small surplus stock that remained in Government hands after the original distribution (46.7).

20. **Messina, Ruins after the Earthquake,** watercolour by Frank Brangwyn RA, c.1910. At first, the Italian government decided to abandon Messina and for two years a permit was required to visit the site. The artist was a regular visitor and his Messina works were exhibited by the Fine Art Society in London in November 1910.
*NMGW, Department of Art*

# SS Drummond Castle, 1896

**21. *SS Drummond Castle*: silver commemorative medal, 1896**
Royal Mint Specimen.
*By bequest (48.126/36)*

This medal may be included here as a small-scale counterpart to the Messina medal. It is a commemorative award by a grateful nation to foreign nationals, in this case civilians, who have gone to the assistance of the British. The liner *SS Drummond Castle* was homeward bound from Natal and Cape Town when at 11 p.m. on 16 June 1896 she struck a reef off Ushant (Ouessant), in fog. Of 246 persons on board, only three survived. A commemorative medal was given in the name of Queen Victoria to 271 inhabitants of Brest, Molène and Ushant for their 'humanity and sympathetic kindness' in rescuing the survivors and burying the dead.

Since 1841 the Sea Gallantry Medal (Foreign Services) had been awarded to foreigners or British seamen serving in foreign ships who rendered services to British ships or seamen. On other occasions, there were rewards of money or silverware. The *Drummond Castle* incident was regarded as a case worthy of a special medal which, like the SGM (Foreign Services) at the time, was worn on a crimson ribbon.

# The Edward Medal

The Edward Medal was established by Royal Warrant on 13 July 1907 to recognise the 'many heroic acts performed by Miners and Quarrymen and others who endanger their own lives in saving or endeavouring to save the lives of others ...' Unusually, it was financed by private money, primarily that advanced by Mr A. Hewlett, a leading colliery owner. There were two classes, represented by medals of silver and bronze, awarded for deeds in the United Kingdom and the 'Dominions and territories under Our Protection or Jurisdiction'. Two years later, on 1 December 1909, a further Royal Warrant extended the coverage of the medal to acts of courage in Industry, including such areas as docks, railways, even farming. Meanwhile (7 July 1909), the King's Police Medal made provision for the recognition of similar acts by police and firemen. Together with the Board of Trade medal for saving life at sea (see 8), these medals were intended to 'cover the whole range of dangerous employment in civil life'. The Albert Medal – a rare and exceptional award – remained the benchmark for acts of the 'highest devotion and courage' but the new medals provided a mechanism for rewarding exceptional bravery which might otherwise have gone unrecognised.

The Edward Medal was the subject of a consolidating Warrant dated 28 August 1917 and was redesignated as the 'Edward Medal in Silver' and the 'Edward Medal'. When introduced, the EM had been promptly dubbed the 'Miners' Victoria Cross', though it was intended to be a lesser decoration than the Albert Medal. In 1917 the Edward Medal in Silver was regarded as 'equivalent to the Albert Medal' (i.e. the bronze issue).

# Henry Everson

**22. Edward Medal, Edward VII, First Class (silver)**
'HENRY EVERSON'
*By private donation (78.54H/1) See also 44*

Henry Everson was the Mechanic at Powell Duffryn Co.'s Penallta Colliery, near Gelligaer, which opened in 1909. He won the Edward Medal for saving the life of a workman named Samuel Barrett, on 12 September 1907:

'In the process of sinking the shaft of the Penallta Colliery, water was being raised from a depth of 345 feet, and a scaffold was suspended in the shaft for the purpose of walling the sides. The barrel containing the water came in contact with the scaffold and broke it from its chains, precipitating it with two men 30 feet into 12 feet of water. Henry Everson, who was at the top of the shaft, heard one of the men calling for help. He also called for assistance, but seeing the urgency of the case descended the shaft at once by a 4-inch pipe a distance of 270 feet. He then found the barrel, which he was able to pull towards him, got into it and was lowered till he found one of the men hanging on a thin wire, up to his neck in water and almost exhausted, his hands wounded. He jumped into the water,

holding the barrel with one hand, and was able to grip the man by the collar and pull him into the barrel. They were then raised to the surface. The second man was drowned.'
(*London Gazette*, 28 February 1908)

The rather makeshift drainage arrangements had resulted from equipment failure:

'Through the failure of a pump sinking operations had to be suspended in No.2 Shaft, and the water had to be drawn in an iron barrel, pending the repairing of the pump. On the 12th of September a circular walling stage made of wood, was suspended in the shaft 95 yards from the surface, by two wire ropes with four bridle chains. The stage when used for walling covered the shaft, but when water was being drawn an opening 9ft by $8\frac{1}{2}$ ft was made in it to allow the barrel to pass through. The stage was raised or lowered by a crab engine on the surface, and the water barrel was raised or lowered by the winding engine.

'The electrically worked pump, which was out of order, was fixed to the side of the shaft near the stage, and a column of water pipes 4 inches in diameter connected to it, was suspended from the top of the shaft.' (From the report of F. A. Gray, HM Inspector of Mines, 3 October 1907.)

Barrett, a married man with six children, was an experienced underground worker. He was twice knocked into the water (the second time by a falling timber) and owed his survival to being able to swim. Even so, weighed down by his pit oilskins, he was close to drowning when rescued by Everson. The body of Frank Steele was recovered only after Everson and others had again descended the pit and removed the collapsed timbers and scaffolding. An inquest at Maesycymmer Police Station on 20 October brought in a verdict of accidental death and a recommendation that Everson's name be put forward for the award of the 'King's Medal for Bravery in Mines'.

This had already happened and Everson's was the first Edward Medal case to be considered in detail by the Home Office. The civil servants were dithering: was the standard of Everson's heroism sufficient for the new medal? 'I think a "handsome letter" would meet the case' (11 October). 'This is not an easy case. Everson behaved with coolness, promptitude and tenacity, and in circumstances in which a man of less nerve might easily have lost his life. The medal however is for cases in which the rescuer runs at least considerable risk of losing his own life – another impression left on one by the experts is that Everson was – thanks to his qualities – not at any time in great danger himself … another point of the medal is I understand to be limited to a comparatively small number of cases' (11 October). 'The difficulty of this case is, naturally, the newness of the matter. I think the case is worthy of a medal' (12 October).

On 29 October expert advice was sought: 'I asked Mr Pickering who happened to be at the Office to look at this … Mr Pickering's note herewith expresses a decided opinion that Everson's gallantry was conspicuous even when measured by the standard of bravery amongst miners and that he exposed himself to serious risk. You will perhaps think this sufficient.
?Recommend to His Majesty Everson for medal of the first class.'

Everson was invested by the King at Buckingham Palace on 27 February 1908. He and Frank Chandler of the Hoyland Silkstone Colliery, near Barnsley, Yorkshire were the first recipients of the new decoration, both of the First Class.

23. **Everson (right) and Chandler arriving at the Palace,** conducted by a King's Messenger. *NMGW accession file*

THE MINERS' VICTORIA CROSS:
THE FIRST PRESENTATION OF THE KING'S MEDAL
FOR HEROISM IN MINES.

24. **The first Edward Medal investiture**
*ILN*, 7 March 1908. Everson looks on as Chandler receives his medal. *Illustrated London News Picture Library*

Since the Royal Humane Society had promptly awarded Everson its medal (see 44), Home Office officials raised the question as to whether it was permissible to wear more than one medal for the same action. A ruling was sought from the King, as a result of which it was minuted that 'where an action for which an Edward Medal is given was done in water in a case where a R. Humane Soc. Medal has been or is likely to be given, that in sending the Ed Medal recipient be informed King's wishes' (10 March 1908). These were, 'that unless the circumstances were very exceptional, no individual should be allowed to wear two medals in respect of the same occurrence.' On 26 March, letters to this effect were sent to Everson, the Royal Humane Society, the Board of Trade and the Liverpool Shipwreck & Humane Society. The ruling applied, in effect, to official occasions, since it was recognised that it would be hard to enforce otherwise. Another result was a move to closer co-ordination between the Home Office and other awarding bodies.

'Mr Pickering', who advised the Home Office on Everson's award, was William Henry Pickering (1858-1912), Chief Inspector of Mines, Yorkshire and North Midlands District. In July 1910, he himself received the Edward Medal, First Class, for his part in attempting to rescue a miner trapped 109 yards down after a scaffold collapsed during the sinking of a shaft at the Water Haigh Mine, at Oulton, near Leeds on 7 May that year: a remarkable parallel to the Penallta incident.

## James Dally

25. **James Dally, wearing the Edward Medal** from the *Great Western Railway Magazine*, September 1915
*NMGW, Department of Industry*

The Crumlin Viaduct, near Newbridge, Monmouthshire, was 1,680 feet (512 m) long and rose some 200 feet (61 m) above the valley of the Ebbw. It formed part of the Taff Vale extension of the Newport, Abergavenny and Hereford Railway, completed in 1857-8. The viaduct was opened on 1 June 1857 and by 1863 was part of the Great Western Railway network.

On 25 February 1915 Frank Potter, General Manager of the GWR, wrote to the Home Office enclosing a report on an incident on the Crumlin Viaduct. He ventured the hope 'that the case may be considered in relation to the Order in Council governing the bestowal of the Albert Medal.'

26. **Edward Medal, Industry, George V, Second Class (bronze)**
'JAMES DALLY'
*(96.16H)*

On 28 October 1914, the viaduct was being painted by Messrs Skevington of Derby, contractors employed by the GWR, using a staging which consisted of planks supported by horizontal timber 'putlogs'. Around 5.00 p.m., as the two men were moving the staging, one of the putlogs broke, precipitating the foreman, C. Skevington, 175 feet to his death in the goods yard below. The second man, Thomas Bond, managed to grip an iron stretcher on the main bridge structure, but was left dangling in mid air.

Bridgeman James Dally, of Crumlin, was nearby, supervising the operation: 'I appealed to Bond to keep as cool as possible & hold on; when I would do my best to save him … The position occupied by him was at least six feet from the gangway. I immediately crawled out from the gangway on to the diagonal bracings (which are 3″ wide) between the bottom booms of the main girders & continued to encourage Bond. I asked him to swing his legs in an upward direction, so as to get them around the stretcher, if possible. This he succeeded in doing. I then got hold of Bond's legs; & told him to move one hand at a time & by that means he was drawn nearer to the gangway & when he was near enough I got a better hold of him, & eventually landed him safely on the gangway.'

According to the *London Gazette*, 'The man would probably have lost his life had it not been for the courage and presence of mind shown by Dally' (16 July 1915). Bond himself had no doubts: 'I was suspended in the air; but if Mr Dally had not been on the gangway at the time, & taken the action he did I could not have saved myself … I owe a deep debt of gratitude to Mr Dally, for had it not been for the encouragement he gave me, & the prompt effort he made, I would have undoubtedly met the same fate as Mr Skevington.'

Dally received the Edward Medal from the King on 12 July 1915. He was the only GWR employee to receive this award. The two photographs enclosed with the GWR report provide dramatic confirmation of the hazards faced by Dally and Bond – and of the dangerous nature of the painting work itself, many decades before the Health & Safety at Work Act. The Crumlin Viaduct was demolished in 1965-6, following the 'Beeching' railway closures.

Dally's medal bears the second, definitive reverse design of the Edward 'Extension' or 'Industry' medal, by Gilbert Bayes, who was also responsible for the King's Police Medal (see 76). Bayes was commissioned in 1911 to provide a new version after criticism of the original design by Kathleen Scott. The 'Mines' reverse, by William Reynolds-Stephens, was better received.

Position where rescue took place

27. **The Crumlin Viaduct,** general view showing location of incident, from GWR report
*The National Archives: Public Record Office, HO 45/10771/275460*

Typical stretcher point where Bond was hanging by his hands.

Bracing along which Dally crawled to rescue Bond.

Typical putlog

Tube of staging suspended below girderwork from which painting was done

**28. The Crumlin Viaduct,** detail of scene of incident, from GWR report

*The National Archives: Public Record Office, HO 45/10771/275460*

**29. The Edward Extension Medal**
first reverse design, by the sculptor Kathleen Scott.

Reynolds-Stephens had declined the opportunity to compete for the Extension Medal. Scott's design was regarded as the best of a poor bunch, and the Home Secretary, Winston Churchill, readily agreed to its replacement, approved by the King and ready for issue in 1912.

*Specimen and photograph by courtesy of the Royal Mint.*

## Arthur Morris

**30. Edward Medal, Mines, George V**
'ARTHUR MORRIS'
*Big Pit: National Mining Museum of Wales, by private donation (2001.1/37)*

'On the morning of the 30th March 1917, a timberman named William Henry Dixon, employed by the Llanhilleth Colliery, Monmouth, was drawing out timber in a part of the mine which it had been decided to abandon, and Morris was assisting him in this work. They had been at work for an hour when, owing to the collapse of a pair of timbers, a fall of roof and sides occurred. Dixon was caught by the fall and fell in a sitting position, being buried up to the neck with rubbish and timber, about eight tons of which had fallen.

'Morris was eight yards away when the fall occurred, and at once responded to Dixon's call for help, and, although heavy stones were still falling from the roof, and Morris was urged by Dixon to stand back, he persisted in his efforts to release his fellow-workman.

'A large stone was then seen to be in imminent danger of falling on their heads, and with commendable presence of mind, Morris ran back 20 yards for a piece of timber, which he fixed in a slanting position over Dixon to support the stone temporarily. Morris then restarted uncovering Dixon, and succeeded in releasing him in about 25 minutes after the accident occurred.

'Dixon was badly bruised and cut all over his body, and while his injuries were being attended to by Morris, who himself suffered from cuts, the stone, which had been supported temporarily and which weighed about two tons, fell to the ground on the place where the men had been, and would undoubtedly have killed them both had the rescue been effected less expeditiously.

'Morris displayed coolness, intelligence and initiative. He was 600 yards from the nearest man working in the mine, and if, as is the usual custom, he had gone for help, Dixon would have been buried by the falling debris and have lost his life.'
(*London Gazette*, 22 January 1918)

In Morris's case, there was an even greater delay, nearly six months, before the Home Office became aware of his actions, in a letter to W. Brace MP, Under Secretary of State, received on 25 September. A minute dated 1 October, suggesting the EM, indicates a positive response to what was clearly a unanimous appeal – from the colliery company (Partridge, Jones & Co.), its employees, and the local Miners' Federation. The recommendation went before the King in early December.

Morris received his medal from the King at Buckingham Palace on 27 April 1918. Arthur Morris was aged 26, and had been an assistant timberman for twelve months, following employment as a collier since the age of 14. Unsurprisingly at that time, he had never been to London and because of his 'very retiring disposition', the Secretary of the South Wales and Monmouthshire Colliery Examiners' Association, W. Frowen, asked that Morris be allowed a companion, a workmate, at the Investiture. The South Wales Miners' Federation, too, hoped to take a delegation to the Investiture, including Morris's father. Both received a similar answer: 'no one except the medallists themselves are ever allowed to attend an Investiture which is held in the drawing room of the Palace. I am sorry that an exception cannot be made, but, of course, there is no reason why you should not all accompany Mr Morris to London. I can quite understand the pride you all feel in the signal recognition he has won' (5 February). A note on the file by R.F. Reynard makes matters clearer: 'The number to be decorated is very large at present – I as Registrar do not now attend these functions, which are carried out with as little ceremony as possible' (1 February). There was, after all, a war on and Morris's was but one award amongst many. Subsequently, invitations specified that 'no spectators will be allowed at the Investiture.' Today, recipients are permitted to bring three guests with them to watch the ceremony, held in the Palace's ballroom.

# The Clydach Vale Dam Disaster

**Robert Ralph Williams**

Water from abandoned mine workings was the cause of another Rhondda Valley disaster, on 11 March 1910. The village of Clydach Vale lies around 5 km west of Porth. Here the Ffynondwyn level of the Blaenclydach Colliery had been worked until 1903, but it was not formally abandoned and blocked until 1909. The water that accumulated was drained through the mouth of the level and a culvert into the Nant Cae Dafydd brook. In October 1909 local concern over the amount of water in the level led Rhondda District Council to intervene and the owners of the land engaged contractors to clear the surrounding workings. But at around 4 p.m. on that Friday, the mountainside seemed to give way, releasing a torrent of water, earth and boulders; nobody had anticipated that the workings by then held around 800,000 gallons of water.

The flood destroyed several buildings and in Adam Street, near the level, a woman, her infant daughter and another baby girl were killed; there were several 'miraculous' escapes. The village school, with over 900 children and 28 teachers, lay directly in the path of the water and debris. Thanks to the quick thinking and resolute actions of the school's headmaster, R.R. Williams, almost all were saved.

On 10 July 1910, the Home Office received a petition, forwarded by the local MP William Abraham ('Mabon', 1842-1922). This comprised an account of the disaster signed by Canon William Lewis, Vicar of Ystradyfodwg, and other senior local figures, submitting that 'Mr Williams' action is worthy of the highest honour that can be conferred upon him.' The text of the petition was to form the basis of the eventual official citation.

After checking with the Royal Humane Society (at this stage not convinced that the action fell within the purview of its work) and the local Chief Constable, a decision in principle was rapidly reached, to award the Albert Medal second class – if not the first – to Williams and to send complimentary letters to two of his staff, Mr Matthew Lewis and Mrs Colville (19 July). However, the Chief Constable of Glamorgan, while heartily concurring that civilians should be rewarded, proposed that two local policemen should also be recognised.

PCs 353 Samuel Hockings and 384 Thomas Thorburn were both involved in the rescue, Hockings at Adam Street, where he was injured, Thorburn at the school. Both, by broad agreement, showed great presence of mind in handling panicky crowds and both worked long into the night, soaking wet. A Home Office hint (18 August) that they might receive the 'Police Medal' was rebuffed by the Chief Constable, who had no intention of nominating them for the King's Police Medal unless or until a previous recommendation of his (which had in fact never reached the Home Office) was dealt with (20 August). The two policemen, like their teacher counterparts, had to make do with letters of commendation (7 December).

In the meantime, a fresh complication: 'Perhaps we may now proceed, but now that the Edward Extension has been established it may be a question whether the Edward first class or Albert second should be awarded' (2 November).

The eventual decision was almost exactly that originally proposed in July:

Whitehall, December 24, 1910

The KING has been pleased to approve of the Albert Medal of the Second Class being conferred upon …
Mr. Robert Ralph Williams, Headmaster of Clydach Vale Schools, South Wales, for gallantry in saving life as
detailed below: -

. . .

ROBERT RALPH WILLIAMS

On the 11th March Mr. Williams noticed a large volume of water rushing down towards his school – a
dam having burst on the mountain side – and realising that the girls' and infants' departments of the
school were in great danger, he at once gave instructions for the boys to be dismissed, and rushed to give
warning to the other departments, but not before the approach to the front of these schools was entirely
cut off by an immense volume of water. His only route was through a doorway between the playground
of the two departments. He unlocked this door and shouted to the children in the yard to make their
escape to the boys' schoolyard, and one class escaped this way. Mr. Williams afterwards opened the back
doors of the girls' department, which all opened inwards, and closed the front door.

Mr. Williams then went to the infants' department, having to wade through a current up to his armpits.
He satisfied himself that there was no imminent danger, provided that the walls of the girls' school could
withstand the force of the water, and decided to take the girls to a slope near the back entrance of their
school; but he found that the volume of water had greatly increased, and had burst in the front door and
broken the lower parts of the windows. He succeeded, however, in entering the school, and finally got
the children out safely, although the water inside the building was now fully four feet six inches in depth.
While the last of the children were being rescued, a wall eighteen yards long, ten feet high and two feet
three inches thick, which had formed a partial breakwater, was swept away, and the increased rush of
water carried Mr. Williams out of the building down a flight of steps, where he was severely bruised and
narrowly escaped drowning. At the bottom of the steps he found about twenty girls struggling in six feet
of water, and these he assisted to safety in the infants' schoolyard.

In the meantime Mrs. Colville, an assistant teacher, and her class were caught in another corner of the
yard, bounded by a high wall, which met the full force of the flood. She and the children were being
whirled round by the torrent, but all were rescued by Mr. Williams, who with a child in his arms, caught
Mrs. Colville as she was sinking and being carried away.

Valuable assistance was rendered by Mr. Matthew Lewis and other members of the school staff.

(*London Gazette*, 30 December 1910)

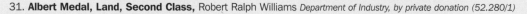

31. **Albert Medal, Land, Second Class,** Robert Ralph Williams *Department of Industry, by private donation (52.280/1)*

It appears that all of the staff responded magnificently and large numbers of colliers, passing on their way home from their shift, also played a valuable part in the rescues. In the event, two girls were drowned and a third died of shock shortly after: 923 lives were saved. A tablet commemorating the event was erected by the Rhondda UDC at the school on 7 December 1910 and each teacher received a parchment certificate which repeated the wording of the tablet. R.R. Williams received his medal from the King on 23 February 1911. Despite its earlier hesitation, the Royal Humane Society also awarded Williams its silver medal (*NMGW 52.280/2*).

That only six lives were lost in Clydach Vale was regarded as little short of a miracle. Inquest verdicts of accidental death reflected the fact that the owners of the level had attempted to remedy a perceived problem. Fifty-six years later, no such luck attended the pupils of Pantglas Junior School, Aberfan, in the Taff valley. On Friday 21 October 1966, a tip of coal waste on the hillside above the school, weakened by springs and by recent heavy rain, collapsed at 9.15 a.m., burying the school and about twenty houses. Of 144 people killed, 116 were children, with five of their teachers. Here again, there had been repeated concerns about the safety of the tip, but nothing had been done and the National Coal Board was rightly blamed for the tragedy.

32. **Clydach Vale,**
the view from the mountainside after the flood
*Illustrated London News Picture Library*

33. **Damaged houses in Adam Street,**
Clydach Vale
*Illustrated London News Picture Library*

34. **R.R. Williams,** fourth from right in front row, with his hands on shoulders of a colleague, at a reunion in 1935
*By courtesy of D. J. Carpenter*

Since 1904, the ribbon of the Albert Medal of the Second Class had been widened to match that of the First Class, but still with two white stripes. On 28 August 1917, a consolidating warrant altered the designations of the two awards. To call any such award 'second class' was no longer thought appropriate, so the lesser award became 'The Albert Medal' and the first class 'The Albert Medal in Gold'. In November 1917 the King, who clearly took a close interest in the medals awarded in his name, queried through his Private Secretary the need to continue with two classes at all. This elicited a heartfelt response from Sir Edward Troup: 'So far as the Home Office is concerned it would be a great relief not to have to distinguish between the First and the Second Class (I use the old terms …); but it would, I think, increase the difficulty of deciding where a medal is to be given and where gallant conduct is to be refused all recognition. Those who just miss the Victoria

Cross may receive the Military Cross or the Military Medal; but there is no corresponding civil gradation' (*HO 45/13631/125008/18*). A lengthy memorandum was drawn up, which resulted in all parties accepting the status quo (12 February 1918).

In 1918, too, holders were authorised to use the post-nominal letters 'A.M.'. This had been proposed for holders of the First Class award as long ago as 1877, but had been turned down because of 'possible confusion with '*Artium Magister*'' [today's MA] (*HO 45/63549A/3*). Even so, the Home Office remained unconvinced: 'We were not enthusiastic about it, but in view of the military precedents and as they said your Department [Admiralty] and War Office agreed, we did not feel able to stand out. It has been decided to allow the privilege, but we are not proposing to issue any public announcement on the matter' (10 July 1918) (*HO 45/13631/125008/21*).

# The Order Of St John

The Order of St John was a medieval military religious order whose members cared for the sick as well as defending Christianity. The Order thrived in Britain until its Priories in England and Ireland were dissolved by Henry VIII in 1540. The revival of the Order as a Protestant organisation in England in the nineteenth century led to the foundation in 1877 of the St John Ambulance Association to train the public in First Aid and in 1887 of the Ambulance Brigade to provide First Aid cover at public events, accidents and in times of disaster. A Priory for Wales was established as a separate entity of the Order in 1918. Today the mission of the Most Venerable Order of the Hospital of St John of Jerusalem, a charity and a Royal Order of Chivalry, is, through its two foundations of St John Ambulance and an Ophthalmic Hospital in Jerusalem, 'to prevent and relieve sickness and to act to enhance the health and well-being of people of all races and creeds anywhere in the world'.

The lifesaving medal of the Order dates from a proposal in 1874 to establish 'a system of rewards for bravery in saving life in accidents in mines and quarries' and was first awarded in November 1875. The medals were originally awarded in silver or bronze; gold medals were struck from 1907. A revised design, featuring tiny lions and unicorns in the angles of the obverse cross, was adopted in 1888.

# William Beith

### 35. Order of St John of Jerusalem, Lifesaving Medal, silver
'WILLIAM BEITH', as mounted for display.
*(80.9H/3) See also 10 and 43*

Five silver medals were awarded in connection with the Tynewydd Colliery inundation of April 1877 (see p.14). The recipients were Thomas Eggrington Wales, HM Inspector of Mines for South Wales, and the four men who were the first recipients of the Albert Medal, First Class for Land Service: William Beith, John William Howell, Isaac Pride and Daniel Thomas. The medals were presented on behalf of the Chapter by Major F. Duncan RA, Director of the Ambulance Department of the Order, at Pontypridd on 4 August 1877, as part of the ceremonies that included the first investiture of the new Albert Medals for land service.

# Albert Gubb

**36.Albert Gubb, c.1926**
*NMGW, Department of Industry, by courtesy of John Gubb*

'On November 12th, 1925 in Cribbwr Fawr Colliery, Ernest Watkins, Henry Lewis and Jenkin John Bowden were buried by a large fall of roof weighing about 50 tons. Albert Gubb, the Overman, was informed and on reaching the scene of the accident inquired as to the position of the buried men and was told Henry Lewis was under his feet. He started to clear the debris and found that Lewis was dead. When he had cleared him to the waist another fall occurred which again completely covered Lewis. Then hearing Bowden call he went to him. Bowden told the Overman that he was pinned alongside a tram. Gubb, realizing that Lewis was dead, proceeded to endeavour to release Bowden. He removed a stone and made a hole about two feet in diameter, but was obliged to retire owing to a further fall. He, however, went in again, telling the other men to keep out of danger while he tried to free the injured man. Bowden told Gubb he would not be able to hold out much longer as there was a stone pressing him down. Gubb spoke to him encouragingly and then called for two blocks of wood which he placed as wedges between the stone and tram. This gave Bowden relief. He then proceeded cautiously to clear around Bowden and after four hours strenuous and heroic work (during which successive falls of roof occurred) succeeded in doing so. The body of Watkins was recovered afterwards.' (From the records of the Order, 26 May 1926.)

The medal was presented to Gubb at a public meeting at Kenfig Hill.

37. **Order of St John of Jerusalem, Lifesaving Medal, second type, bronze**
'PRESENTED TO ALBERT GUBB 1926'
*Department of Industry, by private donation (1999.35/4)*

38. **Cribbwr Fawr Colliery**
from A.P. Barnett and D. Willson-Lloyd,
*The South Wales Coalfield* (1921).
*NMGW, Department of Industry*

# The Carnegie Hero Fund Trust

The Carnegie Hero Fund Trust of Great Britain was founded by the Scottish-born philanthropist Andrew Carnegie (1835-1919) in 1908, following his establishment of a similar fund for the North American continent in 1904; a Royal Charter of Incorporation was obtained in 1919. Born in Dunfermline, Carnegie became king of the American steel industry and the richest man in the world. He sold his empire in 1901 and set out to return his wealth to the people, setting up trusts and foundations in Britain, Europe and America. The Carnegie Hero Fund Trust, based in Dunfermline, is one of five Carnegie Trusts in the UK. Its purpose is to support the families of persons who die in attempting to save life and to reward outstanding bravery, persons injured and persons who have incurred financial loss through performing acts of heroism in peaceful pursuits. In exceptional cases, the Fund awards a large (90 mm) bronze medal, the design of which is also depicted on the Certificate. Since 1908 the medal has been awarded in only 173 out of over 8,000 instances of heroism recognised by the Trustees. As well as monetary sums, and where necessary continuing financial support, the Trust has awarded gold and silver watches, and occasionally other items such as binoculars.

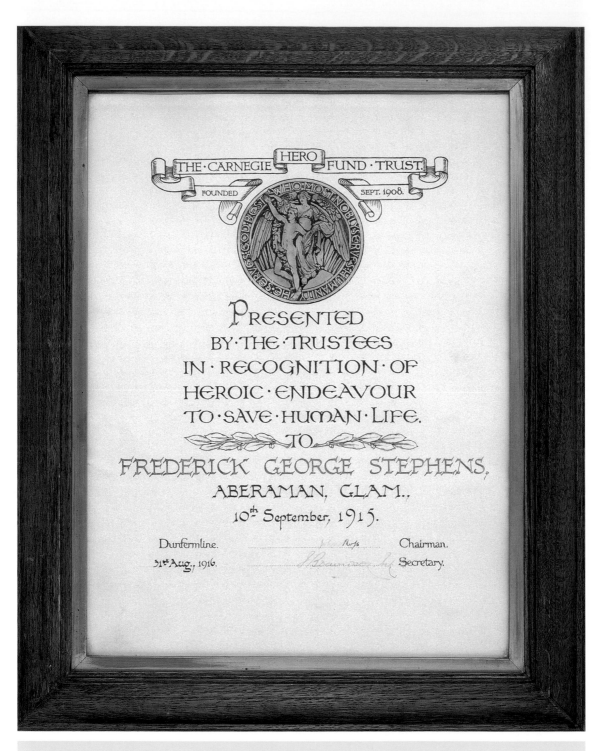

THE · CARNEGIE **HERO** FUND · TRUST.

FOUNDED SEPT. 1908.

PRESENTED
BY · THE · TRUSTEES
IN · RECOGNITION · OF
HEROIC · ENDEAVOUR
TO · SAVE · HUMAN · LIFE.
TO

FREDERICK GEORGE STEPHENS,
ABERAMAN, GLAM.,
10th September, 1915.

Dunfermline.
31st Aug., 1916.

*John Ross* Chairman.
*J. Bannerman* Secretary.

**39. Carnegie Hero Fund Trust, Honorary Certificate framed in oak**
Frederick George Stephens, 1915 (frame size 414 mm x 514 mm) *By private donation (93.81H/1)*

## Frederick Stephens

Aberaman Colliery, in the Cynon Valley, opened in 1847 and closed in 1962; it produced steam coal and in the 1920s had a workforce of 1,095. On 10 September 1915 Stephens, the Under Manager, led a party of four men in rescuing a colleague named Gamble who had been trapped by a roof fall. Stephens protected the trapped man and diverted falling stones for two hours whilst Gamble was freed. Both men were injured, and Gamble was unable to work for two months.

For this feat Stephens was awarded the Edward Medal, Second Class; and the Trustees of the Carnegie Hero Fund awarded him a framed Honorary Certificate and the sum of £20. Other medallists were regularly awarded Carnegie certificates 'framed in oak' and the sum of £20; these include Dally (p.31), Craig (p.66) and Thomas (p.69). The Home Office appears to have written regularly to the Trust informing it of proposed awards. Today, the Trust maintains unwritten agreements with several other recognising bodies, to make each other aware of cases that may be of interest.

**40. Aberaman Colliery, c.1910**
*NMGW, Department of Industry*

<u>EDWARD MEDAL OF THE SECOND CLASS.</u>

<u>MR. FREDERICK GEORGE STEPHENS.</u>

On the 10th September, 1915, a fireman of the Aberaman Colliery, on examining the pit at noon, found some timbers breaking owing to roof weighting, and instructed a workman named Gamble to set props beneath the collars of the timbers.  As Gamble was approaching the spot six pairs of timbers gave way, causing a heavy fall (about 16 tons) of roof and sides, by which Gamble was caught.  He was buried by about four feet of rubbish, his head and feet pinned tight, but his body protected by some fallen timber.

Efforts were made to get him free, but were frustrated by the further falls which were continually taking place.

Stephens, an under-manager of the Colliery, arrived about half-an-hour after the accident, by which time the roof and one side had become so dangerous that no one would venture near Gamble, in spite of his cries for help.  Stephens, however, immediately placed himself over Gamble and called for volunteers.  Four men responded, and, under Stephens's instructions, began to pull down the overhanging stones which Stephens, who is a strong man, diverted from falling on to Gamble, and by so doing was himself injured, though not seriously.

After two hours' exertion Stephens managed to get Gamble free:  Gamble's injuries, though not very serious, were sufficient to render him incapable of working for two months.

There can be little doubt that, had not Stephens stood over Gamble and thus diverted the falling stones, Gamble would have been in grave danger of being crushed or suffocated; and it was Stephens's example which prompted the other men to renew their attempt at rescue, from which, before his arrival, they had several times been compelled to desist by the falling stones.

---

**41. Citation for the Edward Medal**
Frederick Stephens, 1915, headed by gilt Royal Arms *By private donation (93.66H)*

# Albert Gubb

Gubb's actions in rescuing Jenkin Bowden from a roof fall at Cribbwr Fawr Colliery on 12/13 November 1925 are recounted on page 45. The case was reported to the Fund by W. Frowen (for whom see also the case of Morris, p.36) on 16 February 1926 and the Fund's Inspector reported as follows:

'Mr Hughes, Manager, whom I met at the Colliery, spoke very highly of the heroic work done by Gubb during the rescue operations and of the personal risk incurred before Jenkin Bowden was liberated. Mr Hughes was present during a considerable part of the rescue work along with Mr Owens, HM Inspector of Mines, and both give all the credit to Gubb for getting Jenkin Bowden out alive, a statement which was most willingly endorsed by Bowden whom I met later, and who said that had it not been for Gubb's courage he would not then have been alive. Bowden has started to do light work after being nearly 10 months off duty.'

At their meeting in November 1926, the Hero Fund Committee decided to award Gubb an inscribed gold watch, which was presented to him on 8 January 1927 by Vernon Hartshorn, the local MP, at a gathering at the Dunraven Hotel, Bridgend. 'Mr Albert Gubb, replying to the references to his gallantry, said he would have been prouder had he been able to bring about the rescue of the other two men. It was an experience he did not want to go through again, but if anything of the kind happened again he would not be found wanting.' (From the *Western Mail*, 10 January 1927.)

42. **Pocket watch, 18 carat gold, hallmarked Birmingham 1919**
presented by the Carnegie Hero Fund to Albert Gubb (Case 4596)
*Department of Industry, by private donation (1999.35/1)*

# The Royal Humane Society

The Royal Humane Society was founded in 1774 to promote public awareness of the art of resuscitation of the apparently drowned, gaining royal patronage in 1783. Its remit was subsequently expanded to include cases of exceptional bravery in rescuing persons from asphyxia in mines, wells, sewers, etc.

Large (51 mm) medals were awarded in gold and silver. When in 1869 permission was granted to wear the medal in uniform, on the right breast, a smaller size medal (38 mm) was issued.

## William Beith

**43. Royal Humane Society, Silver Medal**
(successful rescue) 'WILLIAM BEITH'
*(80.9H/2) See also 10 and 35*

## Henry Everson

**44. Royal Humane Society, Bronze Medal**
(successful rescue) 'HENRY EVERSON'
*By private donation (78.54H/2) See also 22*

The obverse of the medal depicts a cherub blowing
on a burnt-out torch, with a Latin inscription
'perhaps a tiny spark may yet lie hid' – a reference
to the Society's purpose. The reverse refers to the
saving of life – an alternative version records that
the winner of it 'exposed his (or her) life to danger'
where the rescue attempt was unsuccessful. Beith's
(Case 20,235) and Everson's (case 35,683) RHS
awards supplemented royal recognition by the
awards of the Albert and Edward Medals,
respectively (10, 22). The reverse design – an oak
wreath – is common to many early lifesaving
awards (see also 9, 59). It harks consciously back to
the ancient Roman *corona civica*, the highly-
regarded oaken crown awarded to a soldier who
in battle saved the life of a Roman citizen.

**Royal Humane Society.**

INSTITUTED 1774.

Supported by Voluntary Contributions.

PATRON,

**His Majesty the King**

VICE PATRON,

H.R.H. the Duke of Connaught, K.G., &c.

PRESIDENT,

H.R.H. the Prince of Wales, K.G.&c.

At a Meeting of the Committee of the Royal Humane Society held at their OFFICE, 4, TRAFALGAR SQUARE, on the 10th day of August 1920 Present       General Sir W.T. Adair K.C.B.                                in the Chair

It was Resolved Unanimously
That       Frederick G. Stephens

is justly entitled to the Honorary Testimonial of this Society inscribed on Vellum, which is hereby awarded him for having on the 30th March 1920 gone to the rescue of Trevor Jones who was in imminent danger of electrocution at the Blaengwr Colliery Abraman and whose life he gallantly saved thereafter restoring him to consciousness

President.

F.A.L. Claughton
Secretary.

Chairman.

**45. Royal Humane Society Testimonial on vellum**
Frederick George Stephens, 1920, 245mm x 350mm *By private donation (93.81H/2)*

# Frederick Stephens

In addition to its medals, the Royal Humane Society awards testimonials, on vellum or parchment, and certificates of commendation and for resuscitation. Stephens, already a holder of the Edward Medal (see 41) and now Under Manager at Blaengwawr Colliery, Aberaman, was recognised by the RHS Committee on 10 August 1920, for having saved the life of Trevor Jones, electrician.

'8 PM. 30th March 1920. Blaengwr Colliery. The main switch of the fan supplying air to the Colliery was out of order and Jones in working on it had an electric shock and was burnt. Stephens sprang to him & pulled him back and then applied treatment. Danger of being

himself electrocuted' (RHS, Case 45,480).

The Blaengwawr Colliery was a small 'housecoal' mine that employed around 150 miners. By the 1920s, both this and Aberaman Colliery were owned by Powell Duffryn Co.

Frederick Stephens was born on 22 May 1869, son of a Baptist minister from Ross, Herefordshire. He lived and worked for many years at Aberaman, dying there in retirement, aged 66, on 6 January 1936.

46. **Frederick Stephens** (standing, extreme right), with convalescent miners in 1933
*By courtesy of Miss Margaret Pantling*

# 'My Dear Home Secretary...'

## A case history of the Albert Medal, 1919-20

### Walter Cleall

'I am a chambermaid at the Royal Hotel, Cardiff. On the day of the fire I was off duty and went to my room to have a sleep. I was awakened by the smoke and at once ran out of the room and halfway down the first stairs. I was afraid to go any further and went back into the room and shut the door. I stopped there until Walter Cleall helped me along the parapet into another room. I cannot remember any more.' *Statement of Winifred Jones*

On 12 March 1920, at 10.30 a.m., Guardsman Walter Cleall of the Welsh Guards received the Albert Medal from King George V at Buckingham Palace. The ceremony was the last event of a procedure set in train by two letters to the Home Secretary from a London barrister who chanced to be in Cardiff on Monday 11 August 1919.

13. Aug. 1919

My Dear Home Secretary
Heroic Rescue at a Fire

You may have seen an account in yesterday's Papers of a rescue from fire by a young workman in Cardiff which took place on Monday afternoon and I enclose a cutting from the "Daily Sketch" of today, as it gives his photograph and his name.

My object in venturing to trouble you in the matter, is to recommend the young fellow to your consideration, in the hope that you may see your way to advise his Majesty to give him the Albert Medal or some other suitable recognition of his bravery – for it happened that I was in Cardiff at the time the fire broke out in the upper part of the Royal Hotel, and on hearing of this I hurried to the Hotel, as friends of mine were staying there – and found a huge crowd surrounding the building – and two fire escapes at the fire, both extended to their fullest extent, but quite inadequate to reaching the 6th or 7th floors where the fire was then raging, at the front corner of the Hotel, nearer the Railway Station.

A maidservant was imprisoned on the top storey, her escape by the stairs cut off by the fire, and as the Firemen had manifestly failed to reach her, it was said that she was about to jump into the street, which must have been fatal, as there was no jumping-sheet, such as firemen sometimes use.

Just then I saw a young fellow at the top of the Hotel and heard him smash a window, and in a few seconds I saw him crawling along a parapet that seemed no more than 6 inches wide, and watched him draw the girl, who looked like a bundle of clothes only (I fancy the smoke had by then overcome her) along the ledge, and past an ornamental stone projection, which seemed to encroach even on his narrow foothold, until he reached another window, some distance from the corner which was blazing.

Every second one almost expected to see the man and his burden fall into the street, or that the whole of the roof and parapet would come crashing down – and the crowd held its breath until they saw the man go in at the other window, when a wild roar of cheering burst out such as one seldom hears.

A little later, I saw the girl and her rescuer carried into the street unconscious, and taken to the Hospital.

Shortly afterwards, on learning that my friends were all safe, though their rooms and belongings were burnt out, I had to hurry for the train to London – but I heard before I left Cardiff, that on seeing that the fire escapes were hopelessly inadequate, 2 young men in the crowd volunteered to go to the rescue and that Walter Cleal, a builder's labourer, was the man I saw effect the rescue.

I have seen many brave acts but I never saw anything braver and finer than this. For not only had he dense smoke to contend with, but he must have climbed from the 6th to the 7th floor to reach the girl. I did not see him do so owing to the smoke clouds but heard it said that the crowd saw him climb up the water spout from the 6th to the 7th floor. All the time I was present the part involved was a raging furnace and I should judge the height from the street where Cleal rescued the girl must have been 65 to 70 feet.

I do not know what awards are open to you to submit to the King, but I venture to say that in my opinion, whatever is the nearest in Civil life to the Victoria Cross in military life, was handsomely earned on Monday last just before 5 o'c p.m.

I am, my dear Home Secretary
Yours sincerely and obediently

J.W.C. Kingsbury

14. Aug. 1919

My Dear Home Secretary
Cardiff Fire Rescue

Referring to my letter of yesterday, I beg to enclose a cutting from today's "Daily Mail" giving a photograph of the top of the Royal Hotel – and I have marked a cross X to indicate the ledge on which I saw Cleal (or Cleall) crawl with the girl he saved.

The photograph is quite inadequate for the purpose of showing the heroism of this man – for it gives no indication of the height of the building, and it is taken from the wrong corner – for the fire started at the opposite corner – to the left of the picture.

Had it been taken at that side, it might have shown the 2 Fire Escapes which only reached to the windows below any in this photograph.

The girl was rescued from a room in the sloping roof – which is indistinct owing to the smoke, but above the top windows seen.

I have no doubt that the Lord Mayor of Cardiff or the Chief of the Fire Brigade can give you any details which I have omitted, for you can tell what an impression Cleal's bravery and skill made from the fact that this is the 3rd day that the Papers have mentioned the rescue.

My witnessing it was the merest chance, as I never was in Cardiff before, and was only there on Monday for a few hours.

I am, My dear Home Secretary.
Yours sincerely

J.W.C. Kingsbury

HOTEL FIRE RESCUE.—The Royal Hotel, Cardiff, photographed during the fire from which Miss Winnie Jones, a chambermaid, was rescued by Walter Cleall, a builder's labourer, who climbed along a narrow and exposed roof parapet to reach her. An aeroplane is flying over the burning building.

AFTER THE RESCUE.—Miss Jones (x) being assisted by friends to a neighbouring hotel after her escape from the fire.

*Daily Mail . 14.August.1919*

47. **Cutting from *Daily Mail* of 14 August 1919**
sent by Kingsbury to Edward Shortt, KC, Home Secretary
*The National Archives: Public Record Office, HO 45/10965/387966*

The Home Secretary from 1919-22, the Rt Hon. Edward Shortt, was Liberal Member of Parliament for W. Newcastle – and a barrister-at-law.

On 20 August, the Under Secretary of State at the Home Office wrote to the Cardiff City Police, requesting details of the case 'making clear whether the rescuer ran a serious risk of losing his life' and statements by eyewitnesses. In his reply (28 August), Chief Constable David Williams enclosed statements by all concerned, and went on 'I trust you will recommend His Majesty the King to recognise this gallant deed.' He had also been approached by the Society for the Protection of Life from Fire, to submit the facts of the case: 'I have refrained from doing so up to the present and should be glad to have an expression of the opinion from you as to whether the submission of the facts to the Society and recognition by them would be likely to prejudice a mark of Royal favour.'

Cleall's statement, confirmed by Police Inspector Frederick Pratt, refers to a sloping ledge about 16 inches wide along which he walked for a total of 35 feet to reach the girl, using in part a cornice projecting three inches and in part 'shuting scooped out of the stone' as handholds. On reaching the girl, 'I calmed her, caught her round the waist, she clasped me in like manner, and we got back to the window from which I started by the same way as I had come. As we left the room the roof fell in. If we had fallen when going on the first 5 feet of the journey, we should have dropped into Wood Street, a distance of about 100 feet . . .' According to Acting Superintendent Lawrence of the Cardiff Fire Brigade, 'The largest fire escape, when extended 80 feet, and pitched to the building did not reach the window from which the woman, Winifred Jones, was rescued.'

Two other participants in the rescue were Tom Hill, a seaman who, like Cleall, had come in from outside: '… we went upstairs on to the roof. I found I could not reach her…'; and Carl Stuhr, Second Head Waiter at the hotel. 'At this moment Cleall and three or four men arrived on the scene … I led Cleall and three other men to the bottom of the staircase leading to the 6th floor … The smoke on the staircase was very dense and before we proceeded any further we tied handkerchiefs around our noses and mouths. Cleall then went up the stairs on to the 6th floor, and I and the three others followed but we lost sight of Cleall, and owing to the heat and dense smoke had to retire to the 5th floor. We made several other attempts … but on each occasion we were overcome …' (Stuhr). 'I saw Cleall – one of the men who entered the hotel with me – bringing the girl around on the parapet. I opened the window of the room I was in and assisted them both through the room. The girl was in a dazed condition and Cleall then collapsed' (Hill).

By 26 September, the Home Office had marshalled facts and precedents in a Memorandum.

'…The main facts of Cleall's rescue are borne out by several witnesses – including Mr Kingsbury. The risk of falling is shown to have been very great, the fire very bad on the 6th floor, and part of the roof actually did collapse just after the girl was rescued. Cleall was in possession of neither metal helmet nor smoke helmet.'

The memorandum alludes to two recent grants of the medal but notes that 'In 1911 three fire rescue cases were refused in succession. In all these it is laid down that the Albert Medal is "seldom given for bravery at fires".' (One was refused 'largely on the ground that the man rescued his own daughter, and had received a medal from the Society for the Protection of Life from Fire'.) 'The condition that "the risk to life must have been such as may reasonably have been regarded as exceeding the chances of safety" certainly seems to apply to Cleall when he undertook to carry a semi-conscious adult (and a stranger) round the corner of the ledge, with a sheer drop of 100 feet on one side and a burning building on the other.

? Recommend to His Majesty for 2nd Class Albert Medal.'

An addendum (4 October) then notes 'This case resembles other (non-fire) classes of rescue. Two awards were made in 1911 to nurses who climbed on roofs in pursuit of deranged patients ... There seem to have been no awards for cliff rescues since 1900 ... This aspect of Cleall's action may be taken to supplement his claims in respect of danger from fire alone.'

The case was submitted to the King on 18 November and four days later the Home Secretary was able to write to Mr Kingsbury with news of the royal approval. The award was announced officially on 24 December. The medal, ordered from the Royal Mint on 6 December, arrived on 20 January 1920 'correctly inscribed'. Cleall was offered by letter dated 3 March a choice of the 10th or the 12th to receive his medal. By this time he had re-enlisted, joining the Welsh Guards' Depot at Caterham on the 5th.

A letter of 6 March to Cleall's commanding officer, Major Faulkner, instructed Cleall to report to Room 234, Home Office at 10 o'clock on Friday next (12th). There, he signed a declaration that he had read and understood the conditions attaching to the Decoration 'and I hereby undertake to return the Decoration conferred upon me should I be called upon to do so ...' And so to the Palace for his Royal appointment. The award was entered in the Albert Medal Register on the same day.

Walter Cleall was born in 1896. He had served throughout the Great War. 'Cleall is a modest young fellow, not inclining to be too discursive about his exploit. He was demobilised from the army in March last, having served in various regiments for 4½ years in the Dardanelles, Salonika, and latterly in France. He was slightly wounded while in the Dardanelles' (*South Wales News*, 12 August 1919). He served a further seven years in the Welsh Guards before transferring to the Reserve.

In 1971-2, Walter Cleall was among the surviving holders of the Albert Medal when that decoration was revoked. Along with the majority, he elected to receive the George Cross in its stead, and donated his Albert Medal to the National Museum of Wales. He died in 1983.

48. **Albert Medal, Land**
Walter Cleall
*By private donation (73.25H)*

Mary Street, Cardiff

49. **Cardiff: St Mary Street**
a card postmarked 4 Oct 1910. The Royal Hotel is in
the middle distance, with the window of Winnie
Jones's room visible to the right of the clock
*NMGW, Department of Industry*

50. **Walter Cleall in the early 1920s**
wearing his Albert Medal and his Great War service
medals (1914-15 Star, War Medal, Victory Medal).
On his right breast is the silver medal of the Society
for the Protection of Life from Fire
*Kenneth Williams Collection*

WESTERN MAIL. WEDNESDAY. AUGUST 13. 1919.

## ROYAL HOTEL FIRE RESCUE.

**51. The Royal Hotel, Cardiff, after the fire, showing Cleall's rescue route**
From the *Western Mail*, 13 August 1919.
*The National Archives: Public Record Office, HO45/10965/387960*

**52. Cardiff, the Royal Hotel, 2003**
*NMGW/Jim Wild*

# More Gallantry in the Mines

Two inter-war incidents present us with familiar hazards of underground working: collapse (Bert Craig, 1922) and inrush of water (Thomas Thomas, 1933). The case of Bert Craig is strikingly similar to that of Arthur Morris, but with an extra twist that demonstrates that financial insecurity is ever-present, even for a hero.

# Bert Craig

**53. Edward Medal in Silver, Mines, George V**
'BERT CRAIG'
*By private donation (73.28H)*

On 14 November 1922, a 46-year-old workman named Owen Jones was working on heightening the roof in the Main Haulage Lane at Nixon's Navigation Colliery, Mountain Ash, Glamorgan. He had prepared some temporary timbers for removal by the afternoon shift, once the day horses had left the district for stabling. At about 1.30 p.m., Jones passed through the area to collect his mandrel (a hand tool like a pick), when the whole structure collapsed, completely burying him under 6-12 trams of 'clift and bastard ground'.

Three men who were present set about trying to release Jones, when the roof started working and dribbling over them. Fearing for their own safety, they beat a hasty retreat. A labourer, Bert Craig, came past and was told that a man was buried.

'Realising the danger of suffocation to Jones, Craig threw away his coat and told the men "Bugger the dribbling and those bloody stones about to fall, let's get the man out."[1] He sprang to the spot over Jones ... and with undaunted courage and at extreme danger to himself succeeded in clearing the fall over the man and pulled him to safety. Immediately Jones was extricated another fall of some 6 trams of rubbish fell which otherwise would have certainly killed the injured man and Craig. Craig received an injury to his ankle ... but worked on at great pain to himself.

'Craig has shown great devotion and with extreme courage and danger to himself has saved Jone's [*sic*] life, which to my mind he certainly deserves the Edward Medal.' (From Report by the Manager, J.O. Jones, to Capt. Carey, Divisional Inspector of Mines, 18 Nov. 1922.)

A report by Col. J.A.S. Ritson on 22 November, noting that 'his conduct appears even more meritorious when it is pointed out that he is suffering from the result of a severe bullet wound in the head and any blow might have been fatal', recommended the 'Bronze Edward Medal'. Carey went one better: 'I quite agree ... and having on one occasion had the terrifying experience of working in the conditions described I suggest that Craig be awarded the Edward Medal of the First Class' (1 December).

On 25 July 1923, Craig duly received the Edward Medal in Silver at Buckingham Palace – but by now was, literally, destitute. He had not worked since 14 May, following an accident with a runaway horse at Deep Duffryn Colliery (owned by the same company), and the

---

[1]  By the time of Ritson's report, four days later, this read: 'B— the "dripping" and stones'; a subsequent newspaper account simply read: 'Never mind the dripping...'

54. **Bert Craig, EM**, a studio portrait, c.1923 *Kenneth Williams Collection*

compensation, of 35 shillings per week, had ceased on 16 July. His expenses and the cost of a new suit were met by advancing him £9 from a fund collected for him by fellow workmen. Two days later, at a meeting in Mountain Ash, Craig was presented with a total of £60 (less the £9 advanced), made up of £20 from the ever-dependable Carnegie Hero Trust, £10 from his employers, £10 from the local Workmen's Institute and the £20 subscribed by workmen at the colliery. Craig returned to work on 16 August.

An eventual cheque for his investiture expenses came to £2 11s 8d – well over a week's wages (Craig had averaged £2 2s 1d in the year to May 1923).

Bert Craig was born on 11 March 1898 in south Bristol, the son of a tanner's labourer. The family moved to Mountain Ash when he was five, and his working life was spent in the local collieries: to supplement his wages, he trained as a masseur. He served in the Great War in France and the Middle East and was twice wounded. On 18 July 1972 he again visited Buckingham Palace, to receive his 'exchange' George Cross (see 87). Bert Craig died in Mountain Ash on 13 December 1978.

**55. Royal and Antediluvian Order of Buffaloes**
medal to Bro Bert Craig, 1923; a handsome local tribute *(88.18H/3)*

**56. Edward Medal, Mines, George V**
'THOMAS THOMAS'
*By private donation (73.30H)*

'On the 21st September, 1933, there was an inrush of water in the Brass Vein Slant of the Brynamman Colliery, Glamorgan. Thomas, a collier who was working underground at the time, assisted, at the risk of his own life, a youth who had lost his lamp and who was unable, in the darkness and rush of water, to make his way to safety, to reach a part of the working where several of the colliers had gathered. The colliers then divided into two groups, one group seeking a way out by an airway and another group by a roadway which was flooded and obstructed by a mass of timber and rails which had been washed down by the water. Thomas took up the rear in the group that took the roadway, and when they had succeeded in reaching safety he returned, at considerable peril to himself, to fetch the other group, who then escaped by the same route, Thomas being the last to leave.'
(*London Gazette*, 6 February 1934)

The Gazette announcement provides a condensed account of a confused situation, which followed the firing of a shot at around 11.30 a.m., and the subsequent removal of the loosened coal. It involved fourteen people – colliers and their assistants, who were usually boys or youths. Thomas, aged 21, and his 'boy', Idwal Jones, encountered 14½-year-old Joseph Davies having lost his electric lamp, thigh-deep in water and holding on to a timber, unable to go further. The party that escaped via the obstructed 'bully', or roadway, had to clamber over a four-foot high blockage of stones, silt, timber and rails over which water was pouring, with a clearance of about two feet under the roof. Having reached safety, Thomas then returned by the same route, crossing the blockage twice more before being last out: small wonder that he lost his trousers in the process! The water filled the workings during the course of the afternoon.

The case reached the Home Office from the Mines Department on 3 November. Detailed consideration was delayed until January 1934 ('due to search for precedents and my illness'). Some doubts about whether to award a medal seem, however, to have been set aside by 12 January, and on the 22nd Thomas's name was submitted to the King. On 1 February 1934, the Home Office wrote to Thomas informing him of the award of the Edward Medal. On the 7th, he was summoned to an investiture on 28 February. Like Craig, he lived to exchange his Edward Medal for the George Cross. He died, aged 72, on 19 July 1984.

Thomas also received the Daily Herald Order of Industrial Heroism for this rescue. On 9 June 1923 the 'trade union and labour movement's paper' had announced the institution of a bronze medal and certificate, designed by the sculptor Eric Gill, to be awarded for 'deeds of bravery and self-sacrifice performed by workers in fields, factories and workshops, in mines and at sea.' The award was presented to Thomas and to a second collier, D. Elwyn Davies, at the Public Hall, Brynamman, on 29 November 1933. The Order of Industrial Heroism ceased following the demise of the *Daily Herald* in 1964. In all, 440 were awarded.

**57. Thomas Thomas, GC**
*Kenneth Williams Collection*

# The Boy Scouts

The Boy Scouts were founded in 1907 by Sir Robert (later Lord) Baden-Powell – the hero of the Boer War siege of Mafeking. This was (and is) an organisation of boys aged 11-17, the activities of which encourage mental, moral and physical development, stressing outdoor skills, citizenship and lifesaving. By 1910 there were 100,000 members in the United Kingdom alone and it soon expanded to cater for girls (the Girl Guides) and for younger members (the Wolf Cubs). It was not long before it acquired, in 1909, its own set of gallantry awards, a series of crosses in bronze, silver and silver-gilt. These clearly took as their model the Victoria Cross (though the organisation was not intended as a militaristic one) and it is the Bronze Cross which represents the highest award, for 'special heroism of extraordinary risk'.

# Joseph ('Bobby') Green

58. **Boy Scouts, Bronze Cross;** posthumous award, 'J. R. GREEN 15–5–35' *By private donation (53.415)*

'Gallant attempt to rescue his three year old sister from drowning in a quarry pond at Blackwood on April 12th 1935. He lost his life in the attempt' (*Scouts Citation, 15 May 1935*).

Joseph Robert Green was the ten-year-old son of a miner at Blackwood, Monmouthshire. He was playing with his younger sister Olwen and another girl at the local quarry, which was flooded with about 20 feet of water, when his sister slipped and fell into the icy water. 'Bobby' Green promptly jumped in after her but failed to reach her. Two local men jumped into the water but were too late to save either. At the subsequent inquest, the Coroner praised the 'magnificent efforts' of the boy and the two men. Green was a Wolf Cub – nowadays known as a Cub Scout – at the time.

# Lloyd's of London

Edward Lloyd (d.1713) ran a coffee house that from at least 1688 provided premises for the carrying on of maritime business – including the insurance of ships and their cargoes. Lloyd's *Weekly List* was established in 1734 and by 1774 the 'underwriters' had their own premises in the Royal Exchange. Today, Lloyd's is the world's leading insurance market and the world's second largest commercial insurer.

In 1836, Lloyd's instituted a medal in gold, silver or bronze, to reward those who contributed to the saving of life at sea. Like the Sea Gallantry medal of 1854, the early Lloyd's examples, with a diameter of 73 mm, were not intended for wearing. Smaller medals (36 mm), suspended from a ribbon, were introduced in 1896. Further Lloyd's medals, for 'Meritorious Service' (in preserving vessels and cargoes from peril) and 'Services to Lloyd's' (of a general nature) were instituted in 1893 and 1913.

# John Reinholdt

**59. Lloyd's Medal for Saving Life at Sea, bronze**
'JOHN REINHOLDT'
*Department of Industry, by private donation (71.87l)*

On 18 January 1939 the *SS Ulmus* sent out an SOS: 'Need immediate assistance … On fire. Position 36.14 N. 6.58 W.' The Cardiff-registered steamer (2,733 tons gross), owned by Messrs Wilson and Harrison Ltd, was on a voyage from Nemours (now Marsa Ben Mehidi, Algeria) to the Firth of Forth with a cargo of esparto grass, which was used for making paper. She had a fire in the deck cargo on 14 January, but was able to leave Nemours on the sixteenth. Two days later, off Cap Trafalgar, the cargo in the after-deck caught fire. Her call was answered by the Newcastle steamer *Waziristan*. The crew of the *Ulmus* were forced to jump into the lifeboats of the *Waziristan*, which was unable to go close to the burning ship in heavy seas. All were saved, and were taken to Gibraltar where some minor injuries were treated. John Reinholdt was one of three south Wales crew members of the *Waziristan* honoured by Lloyd's for their part in the rescue.

The medal's obverse was originally designed by William Wyon (the smaller medal is signed by Allan Wyon) and represents the rescue of Ulysses from the sea. Ino Leucothea, a sea-goddess but once the mortal daughter of King Cadmus, appeared to Ulysses in the form of a cormorant. She told him to trust for his safety to swimming, aided by a wonderful girdle made from sea-weeds.

**60. Lloyd's Medal for Bravery at Sea**
'SPECIMEN'
*Two specimens, by donation (45.134/5-6)*

The awards of this silver medal related solely to the Second World War (1939-45). It was instituted, with official approval, in December 1940, for officers and men of the Merchant Navy and the Fishing Fleet in cases of exceptional gallantry at sea in the war. Recommendations for the awards, which came from the Admiralty and from items in the *London Gazette*, were scrutinised by a sub-committee of the Committee of Lloyd's. Eynon Hawkins AM (p.84) and Gordon Love Bastian AM (p.86) were both recipients of this medal, announced in *Lloyd's List and Shipping Gazette* on 3 February and 27 April 1944 respectively. Between 1941 and 1948, 530 of these medals were awarded.

# Civilians at War

## the 'Home Front'

Developments in industry and technology transformed the nature of warfare during the nineteenth and early twentieth centuries. There was a huge escalation in destructive capability, as the development of powered flight and of new weapons such as the submarine allowed the evolution of 'total war', involving as never before the non-combatant civil populations who lived far from conventional battlefields.

Late in 1914, English east coast ports such as Yarmouth, Scarborough, Whitby and Hartlepool were shelled by the German fleet. In 1914, too, Zeppelin airships were used for the first time to bomb a city – Antwerp; and from 1915 there were regular raids on London. During the Second World War, which broke out on 3 September 1939, towns, cities and military installations on both sides of the Channel were subjected to intensive aerial bombardment and thousands of civilians were killed.

The George Cross and George Medal were created by Royal Warrants on 24 September 1940 to recognise acts of 'heroism' and 'great bravery', primarily by civilians, connected with civil defence. The George Cross became the highest civil gallantry award, on a par with the military Victoria Cross, and could be awarded posthumously. Not so the George Medal, which ranked immediately below the 'Gallantry' version of the King's Police and Fire Services Medal. Both could also be awarded to military personnel in cases where a services award would not be appropriate. There were soon plenty of opportunities for awards of the new decorations: the Prime Minister, Winston Churchill, was particularly keen that the George Medal should be widely awarded.

The George Medal is of silver, with a reverse design modelled by George Kruger Gray after a design by Stephen Gooden, symbolising 'St George slaying the dragon on the coast of England'.

## Norman Groom

**61. George Medal, George VI type 1**
'NORMAN GROOM'
*(90.22H)*

On 19 August 1940 a lone German Ju-88 bomber attacked the important, but undefended, Royal Naval fuel depot at Llanreath, near Pembroke Dock. A single direct hit on one of the seventeen massive storage tanks started a fire that was to burn for three weeks, destroying eleven of the tanks and millions of gallons of oil. The fire was fought by around 650 men from twenty-two fire brigades, from as far afield as Birmingham and Bristol. Five Cardiff firemen were killed when a burning tank burst on 22 August and there were hundreds of other injuries. Four further German air raids added to the hazards faced by the firemen.

On 22 October, the *London Gazette*, in the guarded language of the time, announced the award of thirteen George Medals 'in recognition of gallant conduct shown when attending a very serious fire'. (This remains the largest number of awards for a single incident.) 'The fire in question was started by hostile air attacks and burnt for a considerable period. While it was being fought there were further air raids both by day and by night, the firemen being subjected to machine-gunning as well as bombing.' Those honoured included Chief Officer Matthew Acornley of Milford Haven Fire Brigade (though not his tireless equivalent at Pembroke Dock, Arthur Morris) and three

Cardiff men: Fire-Sergeant Daniel James Collins (Cardiff F.B.), Sub-Officer William Brown and Leading Fireman Norman Groom, both of Cardiff Auxiliary Fire Service. Precise details are not given, but the awards were recommended by Captain Thomas Breakes of the Home Office from first-hand observation. One Birmingham and eight Bristol firemen also received the George Medal. Groom, according to the *South Wales Echo*, was a 28-year-old married man, formerly a porter with a firm in St Mary Street, Cardiff, who had joined the Auxiliary Fire Service in 1938, being promoted to Leading Fireman in 1939.

62. **'Gallant firemen'** *South Wales Echo*, 23 October 1940. Left to right: Collins, Brown, Groom (George Medals); Sub-officer T. Fitzgerald, C.A.F.S., Sergeant J.A. Germain, C.F.B (commendations)
*National Library of Wales, by courtesy of Western Mail and Echo*

Hier der Beginn des aus geringer Höhe angesetzten ersten Bombenangriffs auf die
Tanklager vom Pembroke-Dock

The beginning of a first bomb raid on the oil tanks at Pembroke docks, taken at a low
height

**63. 'Tiefangriff: Low-flying Attack!'**
the raid on Llanreath, from *Der Adler*,
the magazine of the Luftwaffe,
3 December 1940
*RAF Museum Hendon*

**64. J.L. Davies, GM**
*NMGW accession file*

# John Davies

**65. George Medal, George VI, type 1**
'JOHN LLEWELLYN DAVIES'
**Defence Medal, 1939–45;**
'JOHN LLEWELLYN DAVIES, G.M.' (unofficial naming)
*(90.21H/1-2)*

J. L. ('Taffy') Davies was another auxiliary fireman, then aged 40, working as a hairdresser in Essex. On 30 September 1940, during a heavy air raid over Chingford, a land mine fell into gardens near his house at 72 Royston Avenue, destroying a laundry and several houses. Davies, whose own house was badly damaged, was off duty at the time, in his family's Anderson shelter. He went straight to the scene of the worst damage, at number 21, where a family was buried in the wreckage.

'Having located the casualties, he burrowed into the debris with his bare hands. He succeeded in reaching the bed and, finding the baby, he passed it out to the Wardens. He then tried to release the other victims. This he could not do unaided and Warden Musgrave volunteered to help him.

'Davies then levered up the debris with his body whilst Musgrave crawled under the bed and allowed himself to be pulled out with the woman on his back.

'Still taking the weight of the debris, Davies, after fifteen minutes, succeeded in releasing the remaining trapped person, who was then drawn to safety.

'Davies was in a state of collapse and had to receive first aid treatment but, when it was reported that another child was trapped, he again crawled under the wreckage and continued working for the rest of the night. His heroic action saved many lives.'
(*London Gazette*, 28 March 1941)

After treating Davies, a stretcher party carried him home. 'You may well imagine my surprise a few minutes later to find Mr. Davies back on the job assisting the Rescue and Demolition parties in the extrication of other trapped casualties. In fact it almost appeared to me that wherever there was a hole, there was Mr. Davies in the midst of it' (from a Stretcher Party Leader's report, 6 October) (*HO 250/17*). Warden Benjamin Musgrave, the 'human stretcher', was awarded the medal of the Order of the British Empire (B.E.M.), Civil Division.

Davies, known locally as the 'off-duty hero', was involved in a number of subsequent rescues. His early death, aged 50, followed a period of ill-health that some attributed to his exertions on that night.

# Thomas Keenan

66. **George Medal, George VI, type 1;** 'THOMAS WILLIAM KEENAN'
**British War Medal, 1914-20;** '102164 PTE T.W. KEENAN. M.G.C.'
**Victory Medal, 1914-19;** '102164 PTE T.W. KEENAN. M.G.C.'
**Defence Medal, 1939-45;** unnamed
*(90.23H/1-4)*

On the night of 2-3 January 1941, Cardiff was the target of a large air raid, involving over 100 German aircraft. Around 8.00 p.m. a stick of incendiary bombs fell on the Anglo-American Petroleum Co.'s depot at Victoria Wharf, Ferry Road. One bomb fell onto the roof of number 3 tank, which contained about 300,000 gallons of petrol. Whilst the Superintendent, E.H. Dixson, collected sand and a shovel, the depot watchman, Thomas Keenan, volunteered to climb to the top of the 30-feet-high tank. Keenan covered the bomb with dirt and kicked and brushed it with his hat off the tank to the ground, where Dixson extinguished it. The bomb had virtually burnt through the top of the tank, which was a mere one-eighth of an inch (3 mm) thick. Keenan, whose hands were badly burnt, 'showed high courage in the face of very grave danger' (*London Gazette*, 2 May 1941).

Keenan, aged 41 at the time, had served in the Machine Gun Corps during the Great War.

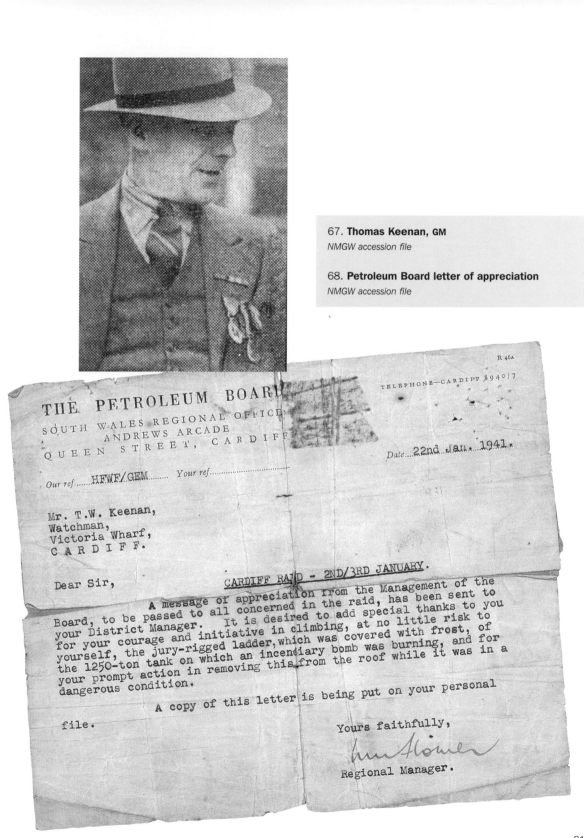

67. **Thomas Keenan, GM**
*NMGW accession file*

68. **Petroleum Board letter of appreciation**
*NMGW accession file*

R 46A

THE PETROLEUM BOARD

SOUTH WALES REGIONAL OFFICE
ANDREWS ARCADE
QUEEN STREET, CARDIFF

TELEPHONE—CARDIFF 8940/7

Date 22nd Jan. 1941.

Our ref HFWF/GEM    Your ref

Mr. T.W. Keenan,
Watchman,
Victoria Wharf,
C A R D I F F.

Dear Sir,         CARDIFF RAID - 2ND/3RD JANUARY.

A message of appreciation from the Management of the
Board, to be passed to all concerned in the raid, has been sent to
your District Manager. It is desired to add special thanks to you
for your courage and initiative in climbing, at no little risk to
yourself, the jury-rigged ladder, which was covered with frost, of
the 1250-ton tank on which an incendiary bomb was burning, and for
your prompt action in removing this from the roof while it was in a
dangerous condition.

A copy of this letter is being put on your personal
file.

Yours faithfully,

Regional Manager.

# They also served: the Defence Medal

69. **Defence Medal, 1939-45** (reverse); unnamed
*By private donation (49.257/1)*

One of the medals of the Second World War was awarded widely to both military personnel and civilians. This was the Defence Medal, given to men and women in Civil Defence, the Home Guard (three years' service), Mine and Bomb Disposal (three months), First Aid, Police, Fire Service, and so on.

The medal's reverse was designed by H. Wilson Parker. In common with other British service medals of 1939-45, the colours of the ribbon are symbolic: green for Britain, beset by bombing and fire (orange) and subject to the wartime black-out. Recipients of the George Cross and George Medal were eligible for the Defence Medal, providing that the decorations were earned for service in Civil Defence. The medal was made of cupro-nickel, and issued unnamed.

# Heroes of the Convoys

Britain has always been vulnerable to naval blockade and in the Great War (1914-18) the German Navy attempted this, using its submarine (U-boat) fleet. This threat was eventually contained by the development of escorted convoys and extensive use of minefields, but thousands of men of the Mercantile Marine lost their lives.

The Second World War's Battle of the Atlantic was of crucial importance, since half Britain's food and two-thirds of her raw materials were imported. Between 1939 and 1945, German U-boats sank nearly 2,800 allied ships, amounting to over 14 million tons; around 750 U-boats were lost, often with all hands. The National Museum's two Albert Medals for saving life at sea both relate to incidents in the early months of 1943, when the Battle of the Atlantic was at its height. The tide was beginning to turn in the Allies' favour, but losses were still considerable.

# Eynon Hawkins

**70. Albert Medal, Sea**
Eynon Hawkins
*By private donation (73.27H)*

'Able Seaman Hawkins was serving in a Merchant Vessel which was hit by three torpedoes and immediately began to burn fiercely. Many of the crew jumped overboard and Able Seaman Hawkins, with the greatest coolness and courage, organised a party of survivors in the water and kept them away from the fire until they were later picked up by one of H.M. Ships.

'Twice he swam to the assistance of other survivors who were in difficulties, himself receiving burns in the face as he pulled them to safety.'
(*London Gazette*, 29 June 1943)

Hawkins, who had joined the Royal Navy in 1940, was serving as a seaman gunner on 'defensively equipped merchant ships'.

The 'Merchant Vessel' in question was the MV *British Dominion*, an oil tanker that formed part of a convoy of fourteen ships en route from the West Indies to Malta. Only two of nine tankers reached Gibraltar, the *British Dominion* being the last ship lost, seventeen of her crew of fifty-three surviving.

Eynon Hawkins came from Llanharan, Glamorgan, the son of a miner, and himself spent his working life in the mines. He was also a professional rugby player after the war and won six Rugby League caps for Wales. He received the George Cross on 5 December 1972, when he was the last Albert Medallist to head the list at an investiture. He died on 17 December 2001, aged 81.

**71. Eynon Hawkins, GC at investiture, 1972**
He is also holding his Lloyd's Medal for Bravery at Sea
*Kenneth Williams Collection*

**72. A tanker explodes after being torpedoed by a U-boat in the Caribbean, 1942**

*Photograph courtesy of the Imperial War Museum (MISC 51235-3P)*

# Gordon Bastian

**73. Albert Medal, Sea**
Gordon Love Bastian
*By private donation (73.29H)*

Convoy SL 126 comprised thirty-six merchant ships, which sailed from Freetown on 12 March 1943, arriving at Liverpool on 2 April. On 29-30 March, the convoy was attacked in the north Atlantic by two U-boats, U-404 and U-662. Four ships were sunk, shared by the two U-boats, and a fifth, though damaged, managed to reach Ireland. Bastian, recently (4 January 1943) appointed MBE for his wartime convoy services, was Second Engineer Officer on the *Empire Bowman*, which sank on the 30th (his 41st birthday), about 350 miles south-west of Ireland.

'The ship in which Mr. Bastian was serving was torpedoed and sustained severe damage. Mr. Bastian was on watch in the engine-room when the ship was struck. He at once shut off the engines. He then remembered that two firemen were on watch in the stokehold. The engine room was in darkness and water was already pouring into it. Although there was grave risk of disastrous flooding in opening the watertight door between the stokehold and engine-room, Mr. Bastian did not hesitate but groped his way to the door and opened it. The two firemen were swept into the engine-room with the inrush of water. One man had a broken arm and injured feet and the other was badly bruised and shaken. Mr. Bastian made efforts to hold them both but lost one, so he dragged the other to the escape ladder and helped him on deck. He then returned for the other and helped him to safety. The more seriously injured man had practically to be lifted up the ladder by Mr. Bastian, who was himself half choked by cordite fumes.

'Second Engineer Officer Bastian took a very great risk in opening the watertight door into the already flooded and darkened engine-room of the sinking ship and both men undoubtedly owe their lives to his exceptional bravery, strength and presence of mind.'
(*London Gazette*, 17 August 1943)

Shortly afterwards, Bastian was invalided out of the Merchant Navy. He moved to Canada in 1947 and received his 'exchange' George Cross from the Governor-General of Canada on 27 November 1973. He died in November 1987, aged 85. In 1990, a new street in his native Barry was named 'Bastian Close' in his honour.

In July 1943, both U-boats were in their turn destroyed: U-662 by American aircraft off the mouth of the Amazon on the 21st (three survivors) and U-404, which had sunk the *Empire Bowman*, was caught by American and British aircraft in the Bay of Biscay on the 28th (no survivors). In just under two years since her commissioning in August 1941, U-404 had in seven patrols sunk fifteen ships and damaged a further two.

74. **2nd Engineer Officer Gordon Love Bastian, MBE, AM, Merchant Navy** by Bernard Hailstone

75. **Merchant ship in Atlantic Convoy, 1943,** by Bernard Hailstone

*© Queen's Printer and Controller of HMSO, 1998. UK Government Art Collection*

# A Policeman's Lot

The King's Police Medal was instituted on 7 July 1909 to reward the Police and Fire Service for gallantry or distinguished service. At first a single design served for both categories, but in 1933 the words 'For Gallantry' or 'For Distinguished Service' were added to differentiate them and the 'Gallantry' award bore additional thin red stripes on its ribbon. The reverse of the medal was designed by Gilbert Bayes, who was also responsible (p.35) for the second, definitive, version of the Edward Medal (Industry). In 1940 the medal's title became the King's Police and Fire Services Medal, in recognition of the bravery of firemen during the Blitz.

# Charles Griffiths

**76. King's Police and Fire Services Medal, For Gallantry**
'C.G. GRIFFITHS, CONSTABLE, CARDIFF CITY POLICE FORCE' *(95.25H)*

Charles Gordon Griffiths was born on 17 June 1902 at Tenby, Pembrokeshire. He joined the Cardiff City Police on 18 March 1924 as Constable, 54C, height 6' 0 ¼", weekly pay 70 shillings (£3 10s, or £3.50). He transferred to B Division as 39B in January 1930. He was awarded the KPFSM for gallantry in the King's Birthday Honours in 1943.

'At 7 o'clock on Tuesday, the 24th November, 1942, a man and woman reported to P.C. Griffiths that a man had jumped into the Ely River. Griffiths went to the bridge over the river and by using his torch was able to see the body a short way away near some bushes on the west bank. He climbed over some railings on to the bank, thinking he could wade into the river (which is here about 88 feet wide and 4 feet deep) and rescue the man, but he found that

the body was drifting downstream towards the east bank. Griffiths went back over the bridge to the other bank, having in the meanwhile asked a member of the public to shine his torch on the water. After making his way through some bushes to a point about 30 or 40 yards from the bridge and below where the body was floating, Griffiths dived into the river, swam upstream and, after two unsuccessful attempts, managed to take hold of the body. He succeeded in reaching the west bank but was unable to get ashore. He was, however, able to hold on to a tree, but became exhausted, and was finally rescued, together with the man whom he had saved, at a spot about fifty yards from the bridge.' (From *The Police Review*, June 11, 1943.)

It was pitch dark and witnesses confirmed that the river, then tidal, was running fast and at the spot where the two men were finally rescued its depth was about six feet: a subsequent report estimated the mid-stream depth as twelve feet. The final paragraphs of a Cardiff City Police report by Superintendent Ivor Jones, 30 November, make it clear that both men survived, and sowed the seed of Griffiths' subsequent award:

'The rescuer and rescued person were both successfully removed form the water. Artificial respiration was applied to both men and, fortunately, both men are still alive. The Constable has since been placed on the sick list suffering from the effects of the effort. The rescued person has been removed from the City Lodge Hospital, to which he was taken after the rescue, to the Whitchurch Mental Hospital. This is the second occasion on which this man has attempted to take his life.

'I would like to draw attention to the following special points in connection with the rescue:

(1) The Constable displayed initiative in using members of the public to assist him in the rescue, viz: he instructed the woman to report to his Divisional Headquarters and to ask for help. This was done through a nearby telephone kiosk as the 'Gamewell' telephone did not appear to be working properly. He used other members of the public to light up the River with his torch, and on this point it must be stated that it was a particularly dark night.
(2) The Constable has done a considerable amount of duty in this district. He knows well that the River bed is not free from obstruction and yet he showed absolute disregard for his own life by diving into the River.
(3) Constable GRIFFITHS is not a good swimmer. He took two years to pass the qualifying examination in swimming. Yet after diving into the water with his boots, trousers and underclothing on and with the water at a very low temperature, he still gave consideration to what was the best thing to do in the circumstances and decided to swim across the river. Under normal circumstances, the distance across the river would not be a hard task, but in the circumstances then existing it might easily have flustered a good swimmer particularly after failing twice to secure the person in the water.

'Statements have been obtained from the witnesses and the medical men who examined the Constable on the particular night. Documents are forwarded herewith for your perusal.

'The rescue from drowning under the circumstances outlined above is, in my submission, worthy of the highest commendation, and I would respectfully draw your attention to the Royal Warrants creating the King's Police Medal. In my opinion, Constable Griffiths displayed exceptional courage and skill in dealing with an emergency' (*Glamorgan Record Office, D/D Con/C 11/182*).

On 17 June 1943, Griffiths was presented by the Watch Committee with the sum of £5 'as a tangible expression of their appreciation of his gallant conduct' (his weekly wages were by now 92/6 or £4 12s 6d/£4.63). He received the KPFSM for Gallantry from King George VI at Buckingham Palace on 6 July.

This was not Griffiths's only notable achievement as a police officer. On 12 April 1945 he was Commended by the Chief Constable for 'the prompt and effective steps taken with Sergeant E. Davies No. 6B in dealing with an outbreak of fire in a railway van at the premises of Thomas Owen & Co, Ltd, on the 8th March, 1945'; and on 8 April 1953 he was presented by the Watch Committee with the Police Long Service and Good Conduct Medal.

There was a price to pay: the latter years of his career were dogged by ill-health. 'Bronchitis' and 'asthma' first appeared in his sickness record in 1943 – not long after the Ely River incident – and regularly thereafter. Having transferred to the CID Firearms Section in January 1951, he took early retirement after 32 years' service, his last day being 17 March 1956. His conduct during his period of service was described as 'Exemplary'. Charles Griffiths died on 6 June 1972.

Between 1910 and 1945 there were eleven awards of the King's Police Medal for Gallantry to officers in Welsh police forces. PC Griffiths was the first (and only) member of the Cardiff City force to receive the KPFSM for Gallantry. In December 1951 the KPFSM was replaced as an award for gallantry by the George Medal, except as an 'equivalent posthumous award.' In 1954, with a new reign, came separate awards: the Queen's Police Medal and the Queen's Fire Service Medal.

77. **Charles Griffiths, 1924**: police 'mug shot' from his personal file
*Glamorgan Record Office D/D Con/C 11/182, by courtesy of South Wales Police*

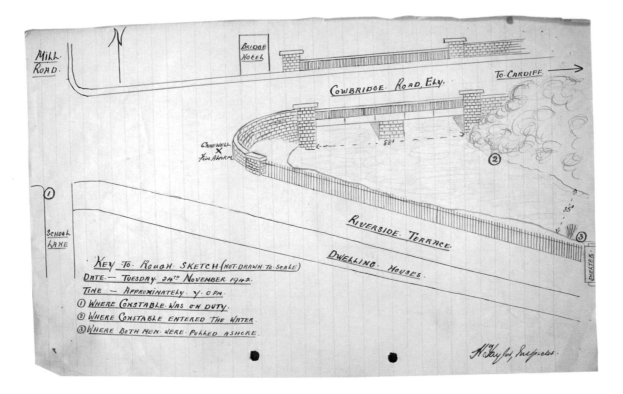

**78. Sketch of the Ely River incident, 24 November 1942**, by Inspector H. Taylor
*Glamorgan Record Office D/D Con/C 11/182, by courtesy of South Wales Police*

**79. The Ely Bridge during the dry summer of 2003** *NMGW/Jim Wild*

**80. Albert Medal, Land**
Kenneth Farrow
*By private donation (73.26H)*

In 1948, history repeated itself, when a young Cardiff Constable, who was not a strong swimmer, dived into fast-flowing waters – in the dark – to attempt to save life, this time that of a child. A new road was under construction over the Cardiff dock feeder.

'On 21st June, 1948, Constable Kenneth Farrow of the Cardiff City Police Force attempted to rescue a four-year old boy from drowning in the Feeder, Pembroke Terrace, Cardiff.

'The incident occurred at about 7p.m. when Constable Farrow was on police patrol duty. He saw a number of persons running, and, on enquiry, was informed that a child had fallen into the Feeder. He at once ran to the place, divested himself of his police clothing, dived into the Feeder and swam underneath a long concrete covering for a distance of about 180 yards in search of the child.

'The Feeder is an aqueduct running under concrete slabs and supplying water from the River Taff to Cardiff Docks. It was uncovered at the spot where the child fell in. The speed of the current was about six miles an hour and, whereas headroom at the end of the concrete covering is 2 feet 2 inches (where the accident occurred) it decreases till it is only six inches. The water is black with a considerable amount of mud or silt at the bottom, and it is not possible to stand up in the water with head above water level.

'Although the child's body was not recovered till later, Constable Farrow greatly exhausted himself in the search and in the ordeal of making his way back against the current, with very little facility for obtaining a proper handgrip. According to witnesses, he was in the waters of the Feeder and underneath the concrete slabs for about a quarter of an hour, in pitch darkness.

'Constable Farrow joined the Cardiff City Police on the 7th February, 1947. He was then a poor swimmer, but he obtained his Life Saving certificate and medallion a few months later. He is not yet a strong swimmer, but unhesitatingly risked his life under conditions which would have daunted even the strongest swimmer.

'Constable Farrow's gallantry was commended by the Coroner and highly praised by the witnesses of his action.'
(*London Gazette*, 6 October 1948)

'To swim against the swift current was impossible. By getting to the side of the feeder and obtaining a hand-hold on a projecting ledge he managed to work his way hand over hand up-current back to the place where he had entered the water.

'He had been under the roadway for 15 minutes. Bystanders, including other police officers on the scene, had given him up for lost.' (From the *Western Mail*, 22 June 1948.)

Initially, Farrow was recommended for the King's Police and Fire Service Medal for Gallantry:

'… one can visualise his difficulties in trying to swim against the stream, running at six miles an hour, with insufficient headroom. Under these conditions, it would not have been surprising if Farrow had lost his life. Mr Welch, Engineer in charge of the reconstruction work, has expressed an opinion that he cannot understand how Farrow managed to make his way back …' (*HO 45/22213*).

It is perhaps not surprising that the Inter-Departmental Committee changed the recommendation to the Albert Medal, which PC Farrow received from the King on 2 November 1948. He received his George Cross on 30 November 1972. Like Griffiths with the KPFSM, Farrow was the first, and only, serving Cardiff policeman to win the Albert Medal.

**Feeder Tragedy Scene**

Police-constable Kenneth Farrow, of the Cardiff City force, indicating the spot where he dived into the Feeder under the new roadway under construction at Pembroke-terrace in an unsuccessful attempt to rescue a boy. (See news story Page Three).

*492 Jamaica "New Li*

81. **PC Farrow at the scene**
from *South Wales Echo*, 22 June 1948
*National Library of Wales, by courtesy of Western Mail and Echo*

82. **PC Kenneth Farrow at his Albert Medal investiture, accompanied by his father and his wife Joan**
*Kenneth Williams Collection*

# The End of an Era

## The last Albert Medals and the 'Exchange' Awards

**Margaret Vaughan**

'*Isle of Tragedy Claims New Victim*

'Three Saved by Boy and Girl Rescuers

'Uninhabited Sully Island, off Swanbridge beach, near Penarth, claimed another victim during the week-end, but was cheated of three more by the heroism of a 14-year-old girl and a boy of 11 who braved a wind-whipped rising tide to reach a party of youths struggling on the submerged island causeway.

'The island can be a death-trap to the inexperienced although it can be used safely by people who understand local conditions. It has a great attraction for adventurous youngsters, but they are often trapped when the causeway to the mainland is covered by the rising tide.

'The weekend tragedy occurred when a party of Scouts left it late to begin their return from the island. They were soon in difficulties with the tide. Thirteen-year-old John Davies, of Connaught-road, Cardiff, reached safety, but although not a strong swimmer went back to assist two friends who were floundering in the rising water.

**83. Albert Medal, Land**
Margaret Vaughan
*By private donation (73.24H)*

'Whitehall, November 1, 1949

'The KING has been pleased to award the Albert Medal to Margaret Vaughan and the Late John Howard Davies for their gallantry in the following circumstances:-

'On May 28th, 1949, a party of Scouts, aged between 11 and 15 years, visiting Sully Island were cut off by the rising tide from a causeway which led to the mainland. Most of the boys got safely across, but two of them were forced off the causeway by the strong tide. The leader of the party returned to help the elder boy but in the struggle he too became exhausted. Margaret Vaughan (aged 14 years) saw from the beach the difficulties they were in. She undressed and swam towards them over a distance of some 30 yards in cold, rough water and against strong currents due to the rising tide. On reaching them she towed the boy to the shore while he supported himself by grasping the straps of her costume and his leader's coat. At about ten feet from the shore a life belt was thrown in which the boy was placed by the other two and the three reached the shore safely. Margaret Vaughan's action probably saved the life of the Scout leader as well as that of the elder boy.

'He was swept away by the tide and his body has not yet been recovered.

'Margaret Vaughan, of Westfield-road, Cardiff, swam out to the two boys, one aged 18 and the other 11, and although exhausted by her battle against the waves and current took them both to safety.'

(From the *South Wales Echo*,
Monday 30 May, 1948.)

'Meanwhile, John Howard Davies (aged 13 years), had safely reached the mainland when he saw that his friend, who was unable to swim, was being forced away from the causeway into deep water. He stripped to the waist and went back along the causeway to help him. By swimming out he was able to grasp his friend and hold him up in the water. Both boys shouted for help and it was obvious that they would not get ashore unaided. By this time a rescue boat had put out from the shore but Davies became exhausted by his efforts, and before the boat could reach them he was forced to release his hold on his friend and they drifted apart. The boat rescued the friend but no further sign of Davies was seen. There is no doubt that in returning to the aid of his friend after he himself had reached safety Davies gave his life in the rescue attempt.' (*London Gazette*, 1 November 1949)

Margaret Vaughan and some school friends had cycled from Whitchurch, Cardiff, for a picnic nearby, when the chaos in the water caught their eyes. The Scouts, too, had cycled from Cardiff:

'One of the rescued boys got on my back while the other one held on to my feet. That was about 40 yards out. There were a lot of people in difficulties with cycles all mixed up. They had been cut off by the tide while wheeling their cycles back from the island' (Margaret Vaughan, quoted in the *Echo*, 30 May). Margaret and her friends had attempted to escape incognito before the ambulances arrived – it appears that their expedition had not had parental approval! – but she was recognised and, on the Monday, became front-page news.

84. **Margaret Vaughan**
aged 15
*Kenneth Williams Collection*

85. **Sully Island** warning sign at landward access to causeway *Author*

86. a. **Sully Island,** the causeway seen from the island at low tide, February 2003; in the distance the tide is beginning to rise *Author*

86 b. **Sully Island** at high tide from the mainland, August 2003 *NMGW/Jim Wild*

The Severn Estuary has the second highest tides in the world, with a range that can exceed 14.5 m. At low tide, Sully Island is linked to the mainland by a broad gently shelving causeway. As the tide rises from the west, a difference in levels develops either side of the causeway and at mid-tide this floods suddenly, giving rise to violent and irregular currents.

'A Swanbridge man told the *South Wales Echo* today: "All the notices in the world, and they are on the land side, will not deter the adventurous. Over the years hundreds have found themselves marooned there for a four-hour wait until the tide has gone down. Some have had to remain there throughout the night..."' (30 May 1949).

*Plus ça change...*

Margaret Vaughan's was the last Albert Medal to be presented to a living recipient. The introduction of the George Cross and George Medal in 1940 had accentuated problems already inherent in the British system of civil gallantry awards. A number of different decorations now existed, the criteria and the rankings for which overlapped. The Empire Gallantry Medal, the gallantry award of the Order of the British Empire introduced in 1922 (not represented in the NMGW Collection) was revoked in September 1940 and its living recipients exchanged it for the new George Cross – now the most senior civil decoration. However, the EGM had ranked *below* awards such as the Albert Medal and Edward Medal!

In November 1949, therefore, it was decided that henceforth awards of the Albert Medal in gold and the Edward Medal in silver would cease, and the AM and EM would only be awarded posthumously. Other situations would be covered by the George Cross and George Medal – posthumous awards of the latter were not authorized until 30 November 1977, by which time there had been other major changes. A new award for exemplary acts of bravery, the Queen's Gallantry Medal, was instituted in June 1974. This medal, which ranks below the George Medal, has been widely awarded. Like the GM it is intended primarily for civilians, though may be given to members of the armed forces.

From November 1968, holders of the Albert and Edward Medals, of any class, received an annual gratuity of £100, but with no new living recipients, these decorations were fast becoming history. The end came with a statement by the Prime Minister, Edward Heath, in the House of Commons on 21 October 1971:

'The Albert and Edward Medals were instituted in 1866 and 1907, respectively, as awards for outstanding gallantry in saving or endeavouring to save life. Since 1949, however, no Albert or Edward Medals have been awarded – except posthumously – and the general public are no longer as conscious as they were of their significance and status. It has been represented that the effect of this is to deprive surviving holders of these medals of the recognition which is their undoubted due. I am glad to be able to announce, with the approval of Her Majesty The Queen, that all surviving holders of the Albert and Edward Medals will be required forthwith to exchange their awards for the George Cross. My right hon. Friend the Home Secretary will now issue advice to those concerned. Pending completion of the exchange they will be entitled as from today to add the initials G.C. – instead of A.M. or E.M. – after their names' (*Hansard*).

Royal Warrants dated 15 December 1971, revoking the two medals, appeared in the *London Gazette* on 6 January 1972. The warrants included the phrase 'the actual medal used for the decoration … may be delivered up to Our Secretary of State for the Home Department for exchange'. The majority opted for exchange, though a significant number held on to their medals. (Of sixty-five AMs, sixteen retained their original awards, as did nine, two of them in silver, of the sixty-eight EMs.) Those who exchanged were given the opportunity to request that their original awards be presented to 'a museum or other suitable body': seven chose the National Museum of Wales. The Museum has since acquired Bert Craig's George Cross.

87. **George Cross** 'Bert Craig 1922' *(88.18H/1) See also p.66*

# Appendix

## Specimen Medals

The NMGW collection contains a number of 'specimen' strikings of medals relevant to this book. A few have been incorporated into the main text; the remainder are listed below. They were all donated or bequeathed during the 1940s.

| | |
|---|---|
| George Cross | *44.37/1* |
| George Medal, George VI, First type | *44.323* |
| Edward Medal in silver, Mines, George VI, First type | *45.71/7* |
| Edward Medal, Mines, George VI, First type | *45.71/8* |
| Edward Medal in silver, Industry, George VI, First type | *45.71/9* |
| Edward Medal, Industry, George VI, First type | *45.71/10* |
| Sea Gallantry Medal, silver, George VI, First type | *45.71/5* |
| Sea Gallantry Medal, bronze, George VI, First type | *45.71/6* |
| RNLI gallantry medal type III, silver, unmounted | *48.126/42* |
| Lloyd's Medal for Saving Life at Sea, silver (2 specimens) | *45.134/1-2* |
| Lloyd's Medal for Meritorious Service, silver (1936) (2 specimens) | *45.134/3-4* |

88. **Display of medals, mainly military, at the National Museum, c.1950**
On the end panel are the Lloyd's specimen medals and others donated in 1944-5, amongst which may be seen the George Cross, George Medal, Edward Medals and Sea Gallantry Medals

# Further Reading

Abbott, P.E. and Tamplin, J.M.A.
*British Gallantry Awards*, London, 1981

Barclay, Craig
*The Medals of the Royal Humane Society*,
London, R.H.S., 1998

Brown, George A.
*Lloyd's War Medal for Bravery at Sea*, Langley B.C., 1992

Carpenter, David J.
*Clydach Vale Flood Disaster 1910*, 1995

Cox, Barry
*Lifeboat Gallantry*, London, 1998

Farmery, J. Peter
*Police Gallantry: the King's Police Medal, the King's Police
and Fire Service Medal and the Queen's Police Medal for
Gallantry. 1909-1978*, North Manley NSW, 1995

Fevyer, W.H., Wilson, J.W. and Cribb, J.E.
*The Order of Industrial Heroism (Eric Gill's Medal for the
Daily Herald)*, London, 2000

Henderson, D.V.
*Dragons can be Defeated: a complete record of the
George Medal's progress 1940-1983*, London, 1984

Henderson, D.V.
*Heroic Endeavour*, Polstead, 1988 (A complete register of
the Albert, Edward and Empire Gallantry Medals)

Jenkins, David and Powell, Moses
*Life from the Dead: being the History of the Entombed
Miners in the "Tynewydd Pit", Rhondda Valley, from April
the 11th until the 20th, 1877*, Cwm-Avon, n.d.

Larn, Richard and Bridget
*Shipwreck Index of the British Isles. Vol.5 – West Coast
and Wales*, London, 2000

Litherland, A.R. and Simpkin, B.T.
*Spink's Standard Catalogue of British Orders, Decorations & Medals*, London, 1990

Llewellyn, Ken
*Disaster at Tynewydd: an account of a Rhondda mine disaster in 1877*, 2nd Edition, 1992

Mackay, James and Mussell, John W. (editors)
*The Medal Yearbook*, Honiton, new edition annually

O'Malley, John D.
'The Albert Medal – a True Classic', *Journal of the Orders and Medals Research Society*, 42(1), March 2003, 29-32

Platt, Jerome J., Jones, Maurice E. and Platt, Arleen Kay
*The Whitewash Brigade: the Hong Kong Plague of 1894*, London, 1998

Scott, Vernon
*Inferno 1940*, Haverfordwest, 1980 (Account of the Llanreath fire)

Smyth, Sir John
*The Story of the George Cross*, London, 1968

Stanistreet, Allan
'Gainst All Disaster: gallant deeds above & beyond the call of duty*, Chippenham, 1986 (Albert and Edward Medal winners who exchanged for the George Cross)

Stanistreet, Allan
'The history of the Albert Medal',
*Journal of the Orders and Medals Research Society*, 40(4), December 2001, 260-5

Wilson, Sir Arnold and McEwen, J.H.F.
*Gallantry: its public recognition and reward in peace and in war at home and abroad*, Oxford, 1939

Wilson, J.W. and Perkins, Roger
*Angels in Blue Jackets: the Navy at Messina, 1908*, Chippenham, 1985

UNPUBLISHED SOURCES

*The National Archives: Public Record Office:*
Board of Trade: MT 9/29/W3202; MT 9/32/M2120

Home Office: HO 45/63549A (Extension of Albert Medal to ... saving life on land, 1877); HO 45/10615/195043 (R.R. Williams); HO 45/10965/387966 (W. Cleall); HO 45/22213 (K. Farrow); HO 45/13631 (Albert Medal: General File, 1905-30)

HO 45/16060 (H. Everson); HO 45/10771/275460 (J. Dally); HO 45/10886/348791 (A. Morris); HO 45/11328 (B. Craig); HO 45/15900 (T. Thomas)

HO 250/17: Interdepartmental Committee on Civil Defence Gallantry Awards: cases 707A (J. Davies) and 713 (T. Keenan)

*Glamorgan Record Office:*
D/D Con/C 11/182 (C.G. Griffiths)

**Wales:** coastal localities mentioned in the text and the pre-1974 counties

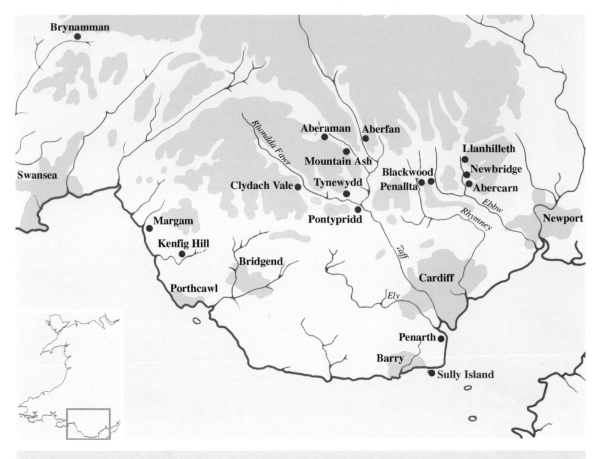

**South-eastern Wales:** colliery, coastal and other localities mentioned in the text